Learning Outside the Classroom

"The power of the outdoors to contribute   educational progress of young people is beyond dispute. The signal contribution of this book is that it helps us translate these powerful learning experiences into mainstream classroom practice. This is an important book – the authors have the great gift of not just being able to link theory and practice but also to provide practitioners with action frameworks to guide their work."

David Hopkins, Professor Emeritus, Institute of Education, University of London

"The practical suggestions and approaches in *Learning Outside the Classroom* will reduce the mystery and increase the ability of educators and others to give children and their families the gifts of nature, to help them live healthier, happier, and smarter lives. Moreover, the authors of this book join a rising chorus in stating clearly and unequivocally that a meaningful connection to the natural world should be considered a human right. Yes, we need more research in this arena, but we know enough to act, and *Learning Outside the Classroom* will help educators, parents, and other caring adults do just that."

Richard Louv, author of *Last Child in the Woods* and *The Nature Principle*

Simon Beames is Lecturer in Outdoor Education at the University of Edinburgh, Scotland. He is creator of the *Outdoor Journeys* programme – a cross-curricular outdoor learning initiative for school children – and a frequent speaker and workshop leader for teachers (in training and practising) about how they may 'take learning outdoors'.

Peter Higgins is Chair of Outdoor and Environmental Education at the University of Edinburgh, Scotland. He is a member of a number of national and international advisory groups on outdoor and environmental education. For the past 10 years he has been a government advisor on outdoor learning and a member of a UNESCO group working to re-orient teacher education to address sustainable development.

Robbie Nicol is Lecturer in Outdoor and Environmental Education at the University of Edinburgh, Scotland. He is a board member of a number of non-governmental organizations, charities, and professional institutes, including the European Institute of Outdoor Adventure Education and Experiential Learning.

Learning Outside the Classroom

Theory and Guidelines for Practice

Simon Beames, Peter Higgins, and Robbie Nicol

The University of Edinburgh
The Moray House School of Education

Routledge
Taylor & Francis Group

NEW YORK AND LONDON

First published 2012
by Routledge
711 Third Avenue, New York, NY 10017

Simultaneously published in the UK
by Routledge
2 Park Square, Milton Park, Abingdon, Oxon OX14 4RN

Routledge is an imprint of the Taylor & Francis Group, an informa business

Cover illustration supplied courtesy of Learning and Teaching Scotland.
Design conceived by Mary Higgins.

Library of Congress Cataloging in Publication Data
Beames, Simon.
Learning outside the classroom : theory and guidelines for
practice / Simon Beames, Peter Higgins, Robbie Nicol.
     p. cm.
  Includes bibliographical references and index.
  1. Outdoor education. 2. Place-based education.
  I. Higgins, Peter J. II. Nicol, Robbie. III. Title.
  LB1047.B37 2011
  371.3'84—dc22   2011012782

ISBN: 978–0–415–89361–9 (hbk)
ISBN: 978–0–415–89362–6 (pbk)
ISBN: 978–0–203–81601–1 (ebk)

Typeset in Perpetua and Bell Gothic
by Keystroke, Station Road, Codsall, Wolverhampton

Printed and bound in the United States of America on acid-free
paper by Walsworth Publishing Company, Marceline, MO.

Contents

Foreword

Learning Outside the Classroom provides a valuable service to educators and others. It moves us forward by providing a solid framework of principles that educators, lawmakers, and others around the world can use as they build their outdoors-related learning programs – and not a moment too soon.

In recent years, the widening gap between children and the natural world, and the benefits of nature for young and old, have come into sharp focus. Children today face unprecedented barriers to daily, meaningful experience in the natural world. Now, after years of neglect in the academic community, research has begun to emerge that reflects both the deficit and the benefits of nature time for children and adults. In *Last Child in the Woods*, I introduced the term nature-deficit disorder, not as a medical diagnosis, but as a way to describe the growing gap between nature and human beings. By its broadest interpretation, nature-deficit disorder is an atrophied awareness, a diminished ability to find meaning in the life that surrounds us, whatever form it takes. This shrinkage of our lives has a direct impact on our physical, mental, and societal health.

At the same time that we are identifying the deficit of nature experience, science is also revealing how time spent in the natural world can help build physical and emotional fitness. We know nature-based therapy has had success healing patients who had not responded to treatment. Studies show exposure to natural environments enhances the ability to cope with and recover from stress, illness, and injury. There now are established methods of nature-based therapy (including ecopsychology, wilderness, horticultural, and animal-assisted therapy among others) that have success healing patients. These approaches will grow in popularity in coming years, including among the traditional health professions.

To health and well-being, we now add intelligence and creativity. New research suggests that exposure to the living world can enhance intelligence for some people. A more natural environment seems to stimulate children's and adults' ability to pay attention, think clearly, and be more creative. One reason may be that, when truly present in nature, we use all our senses at the same time, which is the optimum state of learning.

Thanks to a rich collection of hands-on examples, this book will serve as a commonsense guide for changing individual and institutional approaches to learning and health: how to incorporate local landscapes into course work; how to make certain that students learn safely outdoors; how to balance risk with the immense gains that can be made by incorporating more nature into the educational process and everyday life; how to satisfy the educational expectations of school administrators and the wider community. The practical suggestions and approaches in *Learning Outside the Classroom* will reduce the mystery and increase the ability of educators and others to give children and their families the gifts of nature, to help them live healthier, happier, and smarter lives. Moreover, the authors of this book join a rising chorus in stating clearly and unequivocally that a meaningful connection to the natural world should be considered a human right. Yes, we need more research in this arena, but we know enough to act, and *Learning Outside the Classroom* will help educators, parents, and other caring adults do just that.

Richard Louv, author of *Last Child in the Woods* and *The Nature Principle*

Preface

Within a generation the frequency, duration, and quality of young people's outdoor experiences (both through school and out-of-school) have, in most countries in the world, reduced dramatically. As will become evident later in this book, such changes are not without negative consequences for people's health and well-being as well as their relationships with their communities and planet. The neglect of real-world, curricular learning disadvantages young people as they negotiate an increasingly complex, changing and inter-disciplinary world. This book is our contribution to stemming this tide by providing a coherent rationale for outdoor learning, clear summaries of theory and examples of good practice. Most of all, it is intended to offer teachers support and encouragement as they take the curriculum and their students outside.

In our training, and in much of our own professional practice, we have seen our role as providing outdoor educational experiences that integrate 'personal and social development', 'environmental education', and skills in 'adventure activities'.[1] This model continues to be relevant to worthwhile field trips, residential programmes, and expeditions that take place away from the school.

In recent years, however, we have noticed increasing interest among teachers, parents, and politicians in the opportunities for outdoor learning that schools might provide closer to home. In essence, more and more educators are expressing a desire to bring the curriculum alive by walking outside the

---

1 See more at www.education.ed.ac.uk/outdoored/philosophy.html

school building and into the 'real world'. This developing focus is happening alongside growth in research that provides evidence of the academic, social, and personal (including health and well-being) importance of learning outside the classroom. In essence, the big question in the outdoor learning sector has moved from 'does it work?' to 'how do we do it?' Addressing this issue has been a key motivation for us in writing this book.

All schools are located within geographical, environmental, and social contexts. This book explores the ways in which these contexts can be used to deliver the formal and informal curriculum. Many teachers we know want to integrate outdoor learning into their teaching, but perceive that there are countless obstacles to first overcome, such as bureaucratic paperwork, inclement weather, high student/adult ratios, expensive transport, risk management, and a lack of training. We hope to address all of these obstacles by offering a strong rationale, clear guidelines, and practical suggestions.

WHO IS THIS BOOK FOR?

This book is written for practising teachers and teachers-in-training. It will also be valuable for other education professionals, instructors, parent helpers, and facilitators who are interested in locating their work outdoors and in a curricular context. In fact, we also recommend this book to teachers who are *not* interested in taking their classes outside! We hope that policy writers, curriculum planners, and even politicians will take some notice of the content because, as we have made clear in the book, outdoor learning experiences can play a significant role in the education of our young people. Although many of the guidelines will be useful for teachers of all school levels, there is an obvious slant towards upper primary/early secondary contexts.

As we explain in the following chapter, there are four main areas in which learning outside the classroom generally takes place. This book covers the first two: the school grounds and the local neighbourhood or community. In these two areas, students can normally walk or take public transport to all sites of learning.

Curricular outdoor learning is facilitated by teachers who draw upon circumstances and people from the local community. Unlike the popular tradition of going to a residential outdoor centre, the instructors, activities, and equipment are not 'bought' as if they were a commodity. While we fully support the important work provided by residential centres, a point central to our argument is that, for reasons that will become clear, young people need to know their own place first, before being transported to somewhere far away – especially for their initial outdoor learning experiences.

OUR PLANET AND OUR PEOPLE

One assumption that appears to pervade most Initial Teacher Education programmes is that learning happens indoors. One only has to examine programme calendars and prospectuses from teacher training institutions to see this. Ask teachers, parents, and students whether they think a child can reach his or her full capacity to learn and contribute to society if they are confined to the four walls of their school building for the entirety of their formal education, and you will probably get a resounding 'of course not' as your answer.

It follows that if we want people to live well in this world (Orr, 2004), they need to be educated in this world – in our gardens, green-spaces, local businesses, and municipal governments. We are not saying 'good bye' to our classrooms; we are opening them up to the world outside!

Broadly speaking, there are two educational imperatives within the pages that follow. The first is to educate the whole child in authentic, hands-on learning contexts in the real world. The second concerns helping our fragile planet and weakened communities be restored and cared for by engaged, energetic young people.

Richard Louv (2008) writes that 'Our society is teaching young people to avoid direct experience in nature' (p. 2). Increasingly, the media reinforces the beliefs that what is outside the home or the school will hurt us and that nature is 'other'.

All of this comes back to the importance of authentic learning contexts: learning in the 'real world', and not through contrived academic exercises that are used in 'preparation' for entry into the real world. Sure, our classrooms may be the 'headquarters' for learning, but if our young people are to reach their full capacity as humans and the planet is to flourish under their stewardship, then they must understand firsthand how to grow food; how food webs work; where rubbish and sewage ends up; how citizens can exert power to address community issues; how to run a small business; the possible global consequences of local actions – and the list goes on. All of these examples require the application of literacy and numeracy skills in 'real world' contexts.

HOW TO USE THIS BOOK

'Learning outdoors' has deliberately been written without a lot of specific activities that can be cut and pasted to other contexts. So, rather than being a recipe book, what follows is a collection of principles and guidelines to be considered and then used to inform an integrated, holistic approach to teaching that has unique relevance to the cultures and communities, as well as the landscapes and ecosystems in which students live and go to school. The notion of a specific 'how to' book is incompatible with the tenets of learning that pay specific attention to people's places. Therefore, the case studies provided at the end of each chapter should be seen as illustrative rather than prescriptive.

As with all ideas and thinking, the contents of this book may be contentious and may require updating in the future. That is fine with us; we genuinely welcome any feedback that readers can offer. Perhaps most of all, we encourage teachers to use this book as a means of critically reflecting on their practice. Is there a more meaningful way to teach and learn? We challenge you to explore options of what might be!

Finally, we do not believe that outdoor learning is the answer to the ills of mainstream education. We have seen much indoor teaching that is exemplary and lots of outdoor teaching that is poor. In the end, this is not about outdoor *versus* indoor education; this is about good teaching. Good teaching involves being in the classroom, in the school grounds, in the local community – wherever appropriate. The 'where appropriate' part is the area of ambiguity that teachers must face, particularly in the absence of a recipe book.

We wish you well in your teaching – both indoors and outdoors.

Acknowledgements

We are indebted to colleagues, friends, and graduate students from around the globe, who over many years have influenced and challenged our thinking and practice. We thank the following people for the time they took to make careful and constructive comment on the manuscript:

Peter Bentsen
Jennifer Broughton
Alastair Davidson
Tom Drake
Tim Gill
Charles 'Reb' Gregg
Sam Harrison
Frances Kennedy
Edmund Lim

Grant Linney
Peter Martin
Ally Morgan
Cindy Ng
Juliet Robertson
Shang Thian Huat
Chalmers Smith
Scott Taylor
Glyn Thomas

Finally, we would like to thank Richard Louv for agreeing to write the Foreword, and Naomi Silverman from Routledge for her patience, support, and guidance throughout the book writing process.

Chapter 1

Introduction and overview

CHAPTER AIMS

- Understand the broad conception of 'outdoor learning', its rationale and its many educational benefits.
- Recognize how school grounds and local areas can become easily accessible extensions of the classroom.
- Become familiar with the four broad contexts for learning outdoors.
- Be aware of eight guidelines that can be considered when planning lessons outside the classroom.

INTRODUCTION

A growing body of academic literature provides a clear rationale for classroom teachers taking their students outside during class time. There are three particularly convincing reasons for doing so: the outdoors provides a means of bringing curricula alive, it helps students understand our environment and related issues of sustainable development, and it encourages physical activity. This third point resonates with a growing body of evidence strongly indicating that time spent in green spaces brings health and well-being benefits, and provides opportunities for children to learn how to evaluate and manage risks.

Significantly, outdoor learning has the potential to integrate these vital areas of a young person's formal and informal schooling. Nonetheless, it appears that despite more and more teachers wishing to engage their students in educational experiences beyond the four walls of the classroom, many are unsure of how to begin. How can they use the outdoors in a manner that minimizes paperwork and organization time, while maximizing direct, hands-on, learning experience?

Steadily increasing governmental support for learning outside the classroom can be found in many countries. Notable examples are the publications *Curriculum for excellence through outdoor learning* (Learning and Teaching Scotland, 2010) and *Education outside the classroom guidelines* (New Zealand Ministry of Education, 2008). These documents and supporting websites encourage teachers and those in training to focus more of their attention on taking their children outside as part of formal schooling.

This situation, however, is not universal. There are many teachers throughout the world who would like to make the case for outdoor learning, yet are within an educational or political context that is not supportive. Indeed, it may be appropriate to consider such situations as a 'movement' that includes many other kinds of educational and health professionals, charitable bodies, politicians, and parents – all of whom see benefits in children and young people spending more time outdoors (especially in the natural world) and having greater outdoor learning opportunities.[1]

Apart from some academic papers and reports, the resources available to support mainstream teachers in their efforts to take learning outdoors are not ideal. For example, if one scours the Internet, there are many examples of teaching science outdoors. However, much of the focus is on specific – often disparate – activities. While these lesson plans may be educational in and of themselves, as stand-alone activities they are less likely to form an integral part of a coherent approach to presenting a larger curricular area.

Where resources are available for teachers wishing to take curricula outside, they are predominantly for early years; resources for teachers of older children are relatively scarce (with the exception of subjects such as biology and geography that commonly have a field study component). Apart from the need for resources for upper primary and secondary teachers, there is a distinct focus on the 'what' of learning outside the classroom, but little on the 'why' and 'how'. Without the 'why' and 'how' knowledge, teachers are less able to construct meaningful, rich, holistic educational programmes.

The aim of this book is to fill this void in the literature, and present mainstream school teachers with the basic building blocks to integrate outdoor

---

1 See for example, Louv (2008); Council for Learning Outside the Classroom (2006); Outdoor Education Australia (2010).

learning into their daily timetable. This book is not full of prescriptive activities that we encourage teachers to copy, as this ignores important local contexts and cultural landscapes. Rather, *Learning outside the classroom* offers principles and guidelines that teachers will be able to adapt to suit the needs of their students in ways that draw upon content offered by the local landscape, urban or rural. In addition to teachers, this book will be valuable to many others who use the outdoors for educational purposes, such as those who work for outdoor and environmental education centres, countryside ranger services, community and social agencies, voluntary organizations, and so on.

Although there are inherent limitations to any book on education targeting a global audience, it is our hope that by focusing on guidelines and principles (rather than on specific, replicable activities), we will leave readers with enough scope to apply their own creativity and adapt what they read to construct outdoor learning programmes that are culturally and developmentally appropriate for their students.

BACKGROUND

Countries like the USA, the UK, Germany, and the Scandinavian nations have rich histories in outdoor learning. When one hears about outdoor education, images of young people engaging in challenging outdoor adventure activities usually come to mind. Although there are some historical examples of outdoor education being used explicitly to reach curricular aims (e.g. Foxfire, n.d.), the vast majority of the discourse surrounds adventure being employed as a means of eliciting some kind of personal growth (e.g. Hopkins & Putnam, 1993). Indeed, in the first half of the twentieth century, much emphasis was placed on 'character building' and developing 'fitness for war' (Cook, 1999). This emphasis on the outdoors as a vehicle for personal development has grown steadily on both sides of the Atlantic and in other parts of the world ever since. We and others would argue that in the field of traditional outdoor education, provision has developed in the absence of a substantial and convincing body of evidence to support it.

A second traditional rationale for educational use of the outdoors is environmental education. The approach to environmental education offered by conventional field-studies centres probably has the strongest resonance with the guidelines offered in this book. After all, field-studies centres exist to provide students with concrete ways in which they can see academic content brought to life. However, this book has a broader focus and intent.

Historically, after personal growth and environmental education, the third rationale has been skill acquisition in adventurous activities: learning to rock

3

climb or paddle a canoe. Programmes such as these can be likened to physical education lessons that focus on adventure skills rather than, for example, gymnastics or soccer. The three strands of outdoor education programmes focusing on personal growth, environmental education, and skill acquisition, whether separately or in combination, all have their place. However, we see these three applications as particularly limiting in terms of what outdoor learning experiences can be.

In our experience, outdoor education in many English-speaking 'Western' cultures has, in the last 50 years or so, become increasingly focused on adventurous activities conducted in highly controlled environments (e.g. ropes courses). These often take place far from the school, have few connections to the school curriculum, and are provided by instructors trained to facilitate these activities using specialized equipment.

There are few research studies of teachers' attitudes and approaches to education outdoors, but certainly in one large study in Scotland teachers reported that one barrier to schools providing outdoor learning opportunities is the assumption that children's formal outdoor experiences should occur some distance away from school, often at a residential outdoor education centre (Ross, Higgins, & Nicol, 2007). So, in this traditional conception of 'outdoor education', time must be taken out of the yearly timetable, buses must be booked and paid for, and attention to aspects of the curricula timetabled at school put on hold. There is also a perception that a child is more likely to be physically harmed, and the thought of completing the associated paperwork becomes daunting.

Programmes of this nature are expensive, require specialist skills, are rarely progressive, and consequently are experienced infrequently by most children. This may represent one kind of outdoor learning, but there are others!

In a recent review of research on outdoor learning, Rickinson, Dillon, Teamey, Morris, Choi, Sanders, & Benefield (2004) found that non-local residential experiences can be effective in fostering participants' personal and social development. Although this was less so in the case of improving cognitive development, the report states that more localized 'school grounds/community projects have the capacity to link with most curriculum areas' (p. 6).

Udeskole (literally 'out of school') is a Danish term that has strong resonance with 'outdoor learning'. It involves regular use of a school's natural surroundings and cultural settings as extensions of the classroom (Bentsen, Mygind, & Randrup, 2009). Examples might include museums, local businesses, parks, factories, and churches. This integrated approach to learning (i.e. indoors and out) has strong links to community- and place-based education movements in the UK, Australia/New Zealand, and North America.

In much mainstream schooling, primary and lower-secondary levels are often better positioned to foster learning outside the classroom than high schools. In most cases, it simply comes down to the way school timetables are structured. Primary education is often delivered by one classroom teacher (with some specialist support, such as a music or art teacher) and without a rigid, fragmented timetable; it can be inherently cross-curricular. Contrast this to subject specialist high-school teachers who have, say, 45 minutes to deliver a prescribed curriculum (usually teaching to an examination). For all the good intentions and enthusiasm of these teachers, the constraints of time and highly prescribed learning outcomes are often perceived as insurmountable barriers to learning outside the classroom. There are inspirational stories of course, of teachers who have joined forces (e.g. English, maths, and science curricula) to offer inter-disciplinary, local, place-based learning.

In many parts of the world, the outdoor learning movement is no longer something driven exclusively by inspired teachers and principals seeking more meaningful ways to experience, learn, and know; governments and school-boards are starting to take a much greater interest in the increased learning opportunities offered by moving beyond the four walls of the classroom. However, this interest needs support if outdoor learning is to flourish. To this end, this book's central purpose is to provide theoretical and evidence-based arguments for developing programmes, and to offer a range of practical guidelines.

In our day-to-day conversations, the terms 'outdoor education' and 'outdoor learning' are often used interchangeably. Rather than espousing a more traditional view of 'outdoor *education*' as something that occurs predominantly at residential centres or on expeditions, we use the broader and more enabling term of 'outdoor *learning*' to cover all kinds of learning that might take place outside of the classroom. So, for the rest of this book we'll use 'outdoor learning' and 'learning outside the classroom' interchangeably, when referring to any kind of curricular learning that is taking place outside the school buildings.

THE RANGE OF OUTDOOR LEARNING PROVISION

The provision of outdoor learning can be thought of as taking place within concentric circles (Figure 1.1). Four 'zones' of outdoor learning exist, with the school grounds placed firmly in the centre. Beyond the school grounds is the local neighbourhood, which can be explored on foot or by using public transport. Day excursions ('field trips') often take place a little further away and usually require some kind of group transport. Residential outdoor centres,

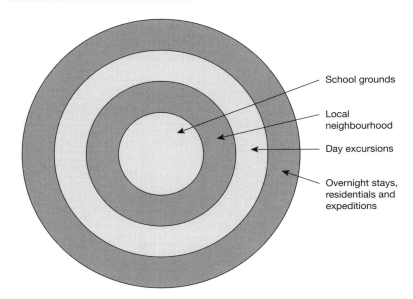

School grounds

Local
neighbourhood

Day excursions

Overnight stays,
residentials and
expeditions

Figure 1.1 The four 'zones' of outdoor learning
(adapted from Higgins & Nicol, 2002, p. 44)

cultural visits, and expeditions that involve being away from home overnight comprise the fourth 'zone', and have their own obvious logistical challenges. For example, any necessary transportation, accommodation, equipment, food and instruction have to be bought, or might be managed by school staff.

This book specifically addresses learning in the first two zones – learning that takes place within the confines of school playgrounds and in local neighbourhoods that can be reached on foot or by public transport.

School grounds are often rich in cultural and ecological stories. The land upon which the school sits has tremendous relevance in the lives of the students, as this is the place where the majority of their formal learning takes place, and for many children, their principal site of unstructured, informal outdoor play and learning.

Some commentators have suggested that our interest in learning outside the classroom partly reflects a decreasing appreciation for the more traditional kinds of 'outdoor education'. We regard all four of these contexts as having tremendous potential for eliciting all kinds of learning. We would argue, however, that organizing trips to far away places without first having an understanding and appreciation of those places that are closer to home needs to be carefully considered. It makes sense that such experiences should be progressive, with the concentric circles being seen as permeable rather than tightly defined zones. Of course, in order to maximize the potential to learn about a given topic, it may be entirely logical to travel some distance in order to experience a contrasting ecosystem or different culture. There will also be value in students 'bringing home' learning from non-local learning experiences and setting this into their local context – perhaps 'seeing it with fresh eyes'.

The model with the concentric rings provides a way of conceiving how we might broadly structure a progressive outdoor learning programme. So, before we venture beyond our immediate surroundings, let us explore the myriad ways in which people, buildings, issues, organizations, and natural world have provided authentic local contexts for curricular aims to be met.

Our emphasis on local contexts resonates with the work of the Scots polymath Sir Patrick Geddes (1854–1932), whose work in education should be seen as integral with his belief in people living and working in harmony with their communities. This belief is illustrated in Geddes' epithet 'place, work, folk' (see Higgins & Nicol, 2011). We have adapted this to define our work as taking place at the conjunction of 'people, place, activity' to remind ourselves of the central significance of this relationship – both philosophically and practically.

GUIDELINES FOR MEANINGFUL AND EFFECTIVE OUTDOOR LEARNING

Learning outside the classroom offers teachers guidelines that can be adopted and adapted to suit their own specific requirements, as well as those of their students, parents, school, and community. Eight chapters outline applicable ideas that will enable teachers to take their students' learning outside. The chapters are briefly outlined here.

Learning across the curriculum

Rather than being regarded as an infrequent, recreational disruption to learning, taking classes outdoors should be seen as an extension of, or indeed integral part of classroom activities and used to meet the curricular and other needs of students. Outdoor learning content can be directly linked to the 'formal' or 'official' curriculum as it is, for example, in Australia (Victoria), New Zealand, Canada (Ontario), Norway, and Scotland. Outdoor learning is a key way of integrating curricular content that, depending on age and stage, is often traditionally taught in separate subject areas (e.g. geography, literature, ecology, and history). There are clear benefits in teaching aspects of these subject areas in an integrated fashion both indoors and outdoors, as this reflects the interdisciplinary nature of the real world – the way we interact with each other and, indeed, our planet. These interactions are also part of the 'informal' curriculum and are a traditional strength of carefully constructed and skilfully guided outdoor learning experiences.

Education for sustainable development

Fundamentally, 'sustainable development' is about developing an understanding of the global implications of our daily actions (e.g. energy and resource use) and taking responsibility for these. However, the lack of direct feedback about how such actions in the 'developed world' can have impacts on some distant place (e.g. a 'developing nation' where sea levels are rising) or some future time, makes it difficult to take sustainable development seriously. Doing so requires developing an ethic of care for our planet, and a willingness to trust (and critique) scientific reports that inform us of such impacts. Developing these skills, and helping students to foster their own personal ethic towards sustainability, is challenging for teachers. While the long-established tradition of 'environmental education' through 'field studies' supports classroom-based understanding of our planetary geophysical and ecological systems, carefully designed and delivered direct, multi-sensory outdoor learning, can also aid in the development of a strong affective relationship with the natural world. The ability to both understand and to care is fundamental to personal decisions about sustainable development.

Learning through local landscapes

Here, students learn about the neighbourhood and landscape – the place – in which they go to school. The story of the land is brought alive by directly interacting with it. This approach to learning can be fuelled by student curiosity, broadened by their own research, and the knowledge gained creatively shared with others through a variety of media. Broadly speaking, learning about the local landscape involves coming to understand the socio-cultural, geo-physical, and ecological phenomena of a landscape – how our culture, the land we live on, and the other living organisms with whom we share the land have been uniquely shaped.

Harnessing student curiosity

In all good schooling, much of the specific content within broader intended learning outcomes is driven by the students, and is negotiated with and facilitated by teachers. Although students are learning within the parameters of the curriculum, they are driven by their own curiosity and are given the scope to focus on specific topics that have high levels of personal relevance and interest. Effective outdoor learning is characterized by its experiential nature. It can start simply by encouraging students to ask questions about the landscape they inhabit or by constructing learning experiences around their interests outside the school building. Helping them to find answers to questions raised by their curiosity enables them to 'learn how to learn' more independently. This allows the teacher to become more of a facilitator than a keeper and 'imparter' of knowledge.

Enabling students to take responsibilities

Students learn by taking responsibility for themselves and others, and by making decisions. Going outside in one's local neighbourhood may not seem as adventurous as going rock-climbing or canoeing, but it may hold much more authentic adventures. The 'broad adventure' offered by student-planned ventures outside the classroom can provide young people with greater opportunities to take responsibility for themselves, others, and the natural environment, than a highly regulated and prescribed 'adventurous' activity found at a residential centre. Students can learn effectively by being in situations that require them to consider different courses of action and then make decisions, the consequences of which will directly affect themselves and others.

Building community partnerships

Effective outdoor learning involves working across social divisions such as age, ethnicity, and race – often through partnerships with community-based organizations that exist to promote the well-being of people and the local environment. Partnering with voluntary organizations, in particular, provides students with genuine opportunities to experience and learn about what it means to be an active citizen and contributor to democratic society, while allowing adults with vast amounts of experience, skill, and knowledge to take on the role of co-educator, along with the class teacher.

Helping older and less able people within the local community is one way that students can make meaningful connections beyond their normal social circle. Community gardening and conservation initiatives are examples of projects that can bring together diverse groups of people in an effort to create a more caring, sustainable social network.

Administration and risk management

All teachers are capable of enhancing their students' learning experiences by systematically and progressively incorporating ventures outside the classroom into their lessons. Learning outdoors does not necessarily require specialist equipment and expert instructors, nor does it require complicated risk assessments. Best practice will involve creating a risk management plan that comprises five basic elements: risk assessment, blanket consent form, emergency action plan, outing checklist, and incident monitoring.

Perhaps most importantly, students can learn how to evaluate risks by making their own assessments of hazards and coming up with appropriate management strategies before each journey outside the school grounds. This chapter emphasizes that teachers should not be trying to completely remove risks; on the contrary, there is an increasing body of literature arguing that educators and students alike should be considering the hazards in terms of risks and benefits.

Supervising people outdoors

Being outdoors with students requires specific management skills, as there are human, environmental, and external factors that require attention. Human factors involve such things as ensuring the students are properly dressed, and adequately fed and hydrated. These controllable factors relate directly to environmental conditions, such as temperature, wind, precipitation, and so on. Finally, external elements such as stray dogs and road traffic can be added to the list of factors that may simply be annoying distractions or more serious health hazards.

Teachers will likely need other strategies for overseeing groups moving from one location to another (in urban and rural contexts), keeping track of who is where, and managing students' primary needs (e.g. food, water, warmth). Teachers will already have their own strategies for effectively managing these elements of day-to-day school life, so it is more a matter of adapting existing practice to the outdoor environment. This requires putting in place systems to ensure that students bring with them whatever they need to be physically comfortable, and, in terms of managing the group, thinking about how to maintain contact and control in a classroom without walls.

These eight areas of meaningful and effective outdoor learning can be considered and incorporated into all teaching plans. Each of these areas is examined in a dedicated chapter, each of which begins with learning outcomes and finishes with guidelines. The final chapter, *'Putting it all together',* also features intended outcomes and guidelines for initial and secondary steps that teachers can take in order to start delivering the curriculum outside the school building.

Chapters 2–9 also include semi-fictional case studies that illustrate how the theory introduced at the start of the chapter can be applied in practice. It may seem a little odd to be making up stories, rather than drawing on real ones. However, we felt that to clearly illustrate the concepts introduced in each chapter, the fictional approach would be most helpful. This allows the case to be written in a way that allows the theory to be more readily adapted to individual teachers' needs.

The decision to use this approach was not taken lightly, and is supported by a growing body of academic literature. Barone (2000) explains how writers using creative fiction are less interested in accurately recreating people, places, and events. Perhaps most importantly, fictional accounts may offer clearer portrayals of situations that can then be used for analysis and discussion (Tierney, 1993). Finally, these cases are not made up 'out of the blue'. The stories are based on the authors 'being there in the action' (Sparkes, 2002, p. 153). The essence of these stories is absolutely real and has actually happened out there in the 'real world'. We are drawing on aspects of these real experiences to create each case study.

LEARNING THROUGH EXPERIENCE

Some years ago, a colleague of ours (Alison Lugg from Australia) was running a university course on outdoor learning designed specifically for teachers-in-training (and this is a true story, by the way). Halfway through the very first class, Alison pulled out a bunch of bananas from her bag, cut them each into four, and distributed them. She then instructed people to eat their piece of banana and describe to the class how it tasted. How would you describe the taste of a banana to someone who had never eaten one? When doing this in class, the closest we ever get to a reasonable answer is that it's sweet.

What's the rationale for doing the banana exercise? It's to emphasize the importance of direct experience, as opposed to gaining information passively through reading or watching a screen. Our children need to 'taste the banana' throughout their educational journey. This has become a useful metaphor in our own teaching, and one that can be expanded to help students consider how the outdoors may offer added opportunities to know things in a variety of different ways – through taste, touch, sight, sound, smell, as well as intellectually, physically, emotionally, aesthetically, and spiritually.

It may seem obvious to state that we humans learn through experience. Indeed, one may learn from one's experience of staring at the blank walls of an empty room, and one may learn from one's experience of designing and building a greenhouse in the schoolyard. What separates these two examples is the nature of the experiences and the meaning that the 'experiencer' finds within them. In most cases, the most effective experiential education pro-grammes are ones that take place in *authentic learning contexts*. These are situations where our teaching and learning takes place in real or realistic contexts and often involves tackling genuine issues, rather than addressing contrived tasks in meaningless settings.

Boud, Cohen, and Walker (1993) explain that much experience is 'so inextricably connected with other experiences that it is impossible to locate temporally or spatially' (p. 7). Learning experiences do not exist in a vacuum that is independent of other experiences. Whether a teaching session features an off-the-shelf, prefabricated lesson plan or an open-ended, generative approach,

> Learning always relates, in one way or another, to what has gone before. There is never a clean slate on which to begin; unless new ideas and new experiences link to previous experience, they exist as abstractions, isolated and without meaning.
>
> (Boud et al., 1993, p. 8)

There are numerous books and articles that discuss experiential learning in the classroom and outdoors. Because this area has received so much attention, we are not going delve deeply into its theoretical foundations, though aspects of its principles will be evident in the coming chapters.

OUR ASSUMPTIONS, BELIEFS, AND LIMITATIONS

Throughout this book, a number of assumptions have been made regarding the nature of education and learning. These assumptions reflect the way we see the world, and cannot help but influence the content.

We believe that outdoor learning:

- is the right of every child;
- can maximize a child's learning across the curriculum;

- has the capacity to elicit personal and social development within each child;
- needs to be strongly linked to education for environmental sustainability;
- rests on universal principles of equality and social justice;
- can provide important opportunities for every child's health and well-being.

Our experience of the field is limited by language and, to some degree, geography. While we have worked in the outdoors in a good few countries, and have professional experience through work-related visits to many more, we are limited by our own experience. Similarly, most of the literature in the field emanates from English-speaking regions with the richest histories of using the outdoors for educational purposes (e.g. UK, North America, Oceania). There are notable exceptions in Scandinavia and Europe (especially Germany). We have done what we can to address this, but fully acknowledge our limitations.

There are many outdoor learning programmes around the world with worthy intentions, but many – particularly those located away from schools and communities – do not directly address content in the official curriculum, and so present a rather limited concept of what learning outdoors can be. Furthermore, the logistical problems associated with outdoor learning that is remotely situated from the school may lead to a perception that these programmes are expensive, infrequent, disruptive to school timetables, and require 'expert' instructors. The emphasis in such programmes is often on adventurous activities and rarely on the curriculum, and so tends to offer the participants and accompanying teaching staff little choice and power, with the landscape being relegated to nothing more than a 'backdrop' rather than a place of inherent learning interest and significance. While thoughtfully designed adventure-based programmes have their place, our intention here is to emphasize a somewhat different conception of the educational use of the outdoors. *Learning outside the classroom* focuses on enabling teachers to bring curricula alive by integrating interaction with local landscape into their practice.

GUIDELINES

- There is evidence of a general transition from traditional, largely extra-curricular 'outdoor education' programmes to a contemporary, mainstream, curricular model of 'learning outdoors'.
- Outdoor learning occurs in four main areas: school grounds, local neighbourhoods, field trips, and overnight residential stays and expeditions.

- Teachers are encouraged to plan learning experiences across the curriculum that focus on sustainability, local landscapes, and community partnerships.
- Effective outdoor learning harnesses student curiosity and demands that students take responsibility for learning that is personally relevant.
- Teachers need to consider how they manage groups outside of the classroom. Furthermore, they will need to be able to assess and manage risks associated with their lessons, so that outdoor learning can become habitual.

Chapter 2

Learning across the curriculum

Chapter aims

- Recognize that there are strong curricular justifications for many aspects of outdoor learning.
- Understand that outdoor learning can support physical, academic, aesthetic, emotional, personal, and social development in schools, and in both the formal and informal curriculum.
- Appreciate that well-planned use of outdoor contexts offers inter-disciplinary learning opportunities in realistic contexts and that these are different (and complementary) to those available indoors.
- Realize how outdoor learning can provide opportunities for planning and decision-making that take student learning into an action context.
- Be aware that a clear understanding of the relationship between indoor and outdoor learning is essential for effective use of the outdoors.
- Be familiar with a range of principles and approaches valuable in planning to make outdoor learning effective in supporting the curriculum.

WHAT IS 'THE CURRICULUM'?

The heart of the learning and teaching experience at any school involves teachers and students interacting with one another with the central aim of acquiring certain skills, values, knowledge, and understanding. Generally, the teacher selects aspects of the 'formal' (otherwise known as 'official') curriculum and helps the student to engage with it, in order to maximize their capacity to learn principles and content. To do so, the relationship the teacher has with the student is crucial, and as we noted in the introduction to this book, so is the authenticity (the 'real-world*ness*') of the learning experience.

The 'curriculum' is generally thought of as the subjects and content comprising a course of study, and as such, is a key interface between the educational establishment, the teacher, and the student. Teachers take the curriculum as advised or prescribed by the State (or other educational body), make decisions regarding which specific elements of content to include, and then develop this into creative teaching sessions. Students have to make sense of this content and place it into their own learning context. They will do so in relation to their interest, their perception of the personal relevance of the content, and what they already know.

While the curriculum is generally prescribed and written down, the approaches a teacher might take and the resources and places they might use are usually left open. Such decisions are made on a pragmatic basis within the context of what is available. So, for example, school teachers generally have classrooms and they use them; they have boards to write on and often computers to convey images and content; they may also use books, posters, laboratory facilities, and so on. Much of this changes if the teacher has access to an outdoor environment and chooses to take their class outdoors. In doing so, *the curriculum has not changed but the context has*, and in making this decision the teacher has to be mindful that this experience should enhance student learning rather than distract or detract.

The term 'curriculum' is often used alongside terms such as 'formal', 'informal', 'explicit', 'implicit', 'null', and 'hidden'. The use of such terms has come about because of a concern among educators that there are implied value-positions in the State's construction of curriculum and in the way a school operates to deliver it. For example, the 'formal curriculum' is what the State (and society) expects to be delivered, and a school's success in doing so is often monitored and reported (by the State, parents/guardians, and the media). The high significance of achievement in formal subject areas is clear, and students, parents/guardians, and teachers respond to this. This type of curriculum is 'explicit' in that it appears in documents that define and guide educational communities – the school, its teachers, and students.

However, a number of authors have explored and critiqued more subtle interpretations of curriculum. Eisner (1985) suggested we could think of curriculum as 'explicit' (as above), 'implicit', and 'null'. The 'implicit curriculum' is what the students will 'pick up' from the way a school is organized and the way teachers teach. For example, if an aspect of the formal curriculum is allocated limited teaching time, or is programmed so that it is an option competing with another subject, the implication is that it has less status. Similarly, the way a teacher sets up a classroom can, for example, imply either control or collaboration. The 'null curriculum' is also important because, for example, when subject matter is left out or an approach or location is not used, they become part of a null (i.e. not visible or acknowledged) curriculum, and are perceived as such by students, staff, parents/guardians, and the wider public.

The term 'informal' is often used in conjunction with 'learning', rather than curriculum, and tends to denote socially mediated, semi-structured learning (e.g. at home and in other social settings) that takes place away from formal educational environments. It is often taken to include language development, developing social skills, and gaining awareness of cultural norms. Although this informal learning tends to be less visible than formal aspects of the curriculum, such learning also takes place within a school. Providing opportunities for students to learn informally is a valid feature of school planning.

Closely related to this is the concept of the *hidden curriculum.* This refers to various aspects of unintended or incidental learning (knowledge and attitudes) that students acquire from their time at school. According to Giroux and Penna (1983), it is the 'transmission of norms, values, and beliefs conveyed in both the formal educational content and the social interactions within these schools' (pp. 100–121) that leads to an attitude or approach to living in society. This concept has been the basis of a number of critiques.[1]

Taken together, these definitional issues are of some significance for outdoor learning. There are aspects of the formal curriculum (e.g. Earth sciences, ecology) where the justification for outdoor learning is straightforward. Furthermore, outdoor settings have long been used for informal learning – especially in terms of personal and social education. In both of these contexts the outdoor environment will be perceived by students as valued by the education system, while in contrast, if the outdoors is not used for teaching or even if the teacher's decision to go outdoors is questioned (*why outdoors?*), this implies a lack of value (null curriculum).

---

1 See, for example, Freire's 'Pedagogy of the Oppressed' (1972), where he considers the subtle, and often considered negative, influence of the state. Also see Gatto (2005) for a more recent American critique.

17

All of this matters because it is an unquestioned assumption that schools operate indoors rather than outdoors (perhaps with the exception of a visit to a local museum, for example), and this message comes across in all aspects of a teacher's life, from selection for teacher training through to possibly becoming a school principal. So, the onus is almost always on the teacher to justify the decision to take students outdoors, while in stark contrast, it seems unthinkable that teachers will ever be asked their rationale for teaching in a classroom (*why indoors?*). This aspect of the null curriculum has consequences for the way students perceive the outdoors, and for their potential to develop a connection with their local environment and love of the natural world (see Chapters 3 and 4).

Why is outdoor learning across the curriculum important?

As with learning inside the classroom, learning outside should be planned in line with curriculum guidelines, in order to maximize the learning potential of these experiences. These guidelines tend to have common themes that consider the content of the curriculum alongside the developmental changes in young people through their years of schooling. Associated structural issues such as inclusion (addressing the educational needs of every child) and transitions (between pre-school, primary, middle school, and high school) are also frequently prominent, as are aspirations to develop cross-curricular understanding, personal and social capabilities, citizenship skills, and informed values.

Around the world, there are several ways in which outdoor learning is related to the local curriculum and social context. It can be:

- *defined as a curricular subject in its own right*. For example, the Australian state of Victoria offers a high-school Outdoor Environmental Studies course (Victorian Curriculum and Assessment Authority, 2005).[2]
- *located in a broader area of study within a specified aspect of the curriculum*. For example, in New Zealand it is located in the area of health and physical education (New Zealand Ministry of Education, 2007, p. 22),[3] and in England it is an option within physical education (National Curriculum, n.d.)

---

2 See Martin (2010), for a discussion of the issues associated with this approach in the development of an Australian national curriculum.
3 Teachers in New Zealand are also supported in taking students out of the classroom and on educational visits, through an extensive website http://eotc.tki.org.nz/

- *related to deeply-rooted cultural traditions* of travel and subsistence, community, nationhood, and recreation. For example, in Scandinavian countries *friluftsliv* (literally 'outdoor air life') is the equivalent of outdoor learning, and is embedded within schools to varying degrees (Henderson & Vikander, 2007).[4]
- *linked to formal curricula,* with many aspects of curricular subject areas delivered outside the classroom.

Each of these approaches has advantages and disadvantages in both the construction of learning experiences of the pupils and also in the potential for teachers and policy-makers to justify outdoor learning in the school. The purpose of this book is not to choose between these approaches, but more generally, to support teachers in taking learning outdoors in a way that is compatible with their own curricular and local context. As implied above and in the footnotes, the justification for outdoor learning in a national policy context is not straightforward.

This tension will be discussed in the following section that refers to work of the Scottish Government, which in 2004 completed a national review of education from ages 3 to 18 called *Curriculum for Excellence* (Scottish Government, 2004). Many outcomes from this review have been adopted and adapted by policy-makers in other countries. There are two main reasons for its inclusion here. First, it outlines a curriculum structure that has an explicit central focus on the learning experience of the student. Second, education policy guidance, extensive resources, and teacher development programmes for outdoor learning have been developed alongside it. Although the explicit linkage between outdoor learning and the curriculum is not unique, it is contemporary and one of few national, state or provincial examples.

The central thrust of *Curriculum for Excellence* is that schools should focus on the development of students' personal capacities that will be valuable throughout life. Hence, the key principles of curriculum design are challenge and enjoyment; breadth; progression; depth; personalization and choice; coherence; and relevance. The principles apply to the curriculum in terms of organization (at national, education authority, school, and individual levels) and in all learning settings. The intended outcome is that all young people should become 'successful learners, confident individuals, responsible citizens and effective contributors' to society (Scottish Government, 2004).

This approach has prompted Beames, Atencio, & Ross (2009) to argue that *Curriculum for Excellence* challenges the 'current emphasis in disciplinary

---

4 See Backman (2010), for a discussion of recent pressures on provision in Sweden.

specialism' and call for schools to 'place the nature of the educated person at the centre of curricular purpose, and to reduce the amount of de-contextualised subject content, and to promote real world experience' (p. 42). Government policy like *Curriculum for Excellence* serves to legitimize the kinds of flexible, cross-curricular, autonomous learning that may be offered by theoretically driven educational opportunities outside the classroom. Beames et al. (2009) highlight that it is 'hard to reconcile this with timetabled, indoor, subject-based, textbook classes' (p. 42). Seen this way, and in the context of the arguments outlined in later chapters, learning outside across the curriculum is a fundamental educational imperative and should be an entitlement for all children.

This view is in accord with the Scottish Government, as outdoor learning is explicitly stated or implicit in a number of recent policy documents that have culminated in the publication of *Curriculum for Excellence through Outdoor Learning* (Learning and Teaching Scotland, 2010). This is the first time in the UK that a specific policy document has issued guidance on outdoor learning. The document is the most explicit recent national policy document we are aware of, and government support is further evident in both the associated website and an extensive in-service training programme. There is no need to consider this document in detail here, as the document itself, its rationale, curricular opportunities, detailed exemplification, advice on planning, suitable locations, health and safety, sources of further support and advice, and so on, are readily available on a dedicated website.[5]

The emphasis we have placed on mainstream curricular planning is not accidental. If outdoor learning is to be respected and valued by the educational establishment, the justifications must be credible. Outdoor learning must be a benefit rather than a distraction or simply 'fun', and clearly must articulate properly with the school curriculum. The use of a local mainstream curricular planning tool is one obvious way of both preparing effectively and 'being seen' to be planning in line with the curriculum. Hence, the principles of *Curriculum for Excellence* have been used to develop our local guidelines in Scotland, and these are now extensively used by schools, outdoor centres, and others in explaining their approach to outdoor learning. In light of the increasing demands on schools to meet high academic standards, such explicit linkage is plainly necessary to maintain support for outdoor learning.

---

5 See www.ltscotland.org.uk/learningteachingandassessment/approaches/outdoorlearning/index.asp

HOW CAN TEACHERS INCORPORATE OUTDOOR LEARNING ACROSS THE CURRICULUM INTO THEIR TEACHING?

The following section provides a number of examples of ways in which teachers can make the most of their local outdoor environments in their teaching. Most of the subject matter here is 'generic' in that it concerns subject matter that exists in curricula all over the world. However, there will be many region-specific variations of this subject matter and other local phenomena that will inspire teachers to use the outdoors creatively.

The physical development of young people is an aspect of both the formal and informal curriculum throughout a student's school life. In early-years provision around the world most nurseries, pre-schools, and kindergartens build outdoor play into the structure of the day. Such activities are generally unstructured, with children being encouraged to make use of playground equipment or the physical attributes of the play area. A well-designed play-ground may also provide many opportunities for physical and sensory development (see Goddard Blythe, 2004). However, more 'complex' environments, such as the uneven ground, logs, trees, boulders, and rocks found in local parks or natural play areas provide additional stimuli for developing activity and the movement patterns that can be transferred to other environments.[6] The outdoor environment is also important for sensory development, as it can engage all the senses and multiple intelligences (Gardner, 1993) in an integrated fashion and in ways not possible in a classroom. This is linked to the developmental role of exposure to 'green-space', which is now well-established as a key factor in health and well-being.[7]

These benefits, together with others, such as improved ability to concentrate in class after spending time outdoors, and improved academic achievement, have been noted and supported by research evidence through other stages of schooling. For example Blair's (2009) review of literature concluded that gardening can have a positive impact on both student achievement and their behaviour in school. While physical activity through play tends to become stylized in the curriculum as physical education and team sports, the role of green spaces remains significant in providing informal opportunities for physical and social development and personal reflection (e.g. Bell, Hamilton, Montarzino, Rothnie, Travlou, & Alves, 2008; Muñoz, 2009).

In their day-to-day work in classrooms, teachers use their theoretical knowledge to help students develop an understanding of subject content.

6 This approach is widely recognized in Scandinavia. See for example Fjørtoft (2004).
7 See Bird (2007) and Muñoz (2009) for reviews.

Judicious use of the outdoors provides excellent opportunities to create innovative practices and experiments that can illuminate theory and provide a real learning context for their students. Consequently, a key over-arching message within this book is that the opportunities for *academic development* outdoors are extensive and can enhance almost any subject area in the curriculum.

For example, the basic skills of reading and writing are often developed from experiences and material drawn from nature. A quick look at the children's reading shelves in a bookshop or library demonstrates childhood interest in the outdoors as a place to encounter nature and adventure. Many teachers make use of this inherent fascination when they set creative writing tasks or bring outside material into the classroom.

History is, of course, concerned with people and place over time, and many aspects of local history are enlivened by visits to a local landscape. This theme is explored in detail in Chapter 4. Historical development is closely linked to the geography and geological past of the area, and it is here where, among the sciences, biology and ecology are most obviously enhanced through outdoor learning.

Studying habitats and ecosystems simply demand direct experience. While curricula may offer examples from internationally famous ecosystems (e.g. tropical rain forests, the great plains of Africa), few teachers can find these just outside their classroom. Nonetheless, the same principles apply around the globe in aquatic as well as terrestrial ecosystems, and it is straightforward enough to find local examples of food chains/webs, adaptation, and competition, and then apply these principles globally. At an introductory level, studies of biodiversity through pond or stream sampling, or rock-pools, seem to have an almost universal fascination. With the aid of magnifying lenses, an astonishing diversity of form can be examined and life and death struggles may unfold in the sample tray alone! With a modest level of knowledge, the attributes that such organisms must have to enable them to live in these environments (such as mayfly larvae hatching to become adults for only a few days before they die) can be interpreted to fascinate the students.

Teaching mathematics outdoors may not spring so readily to mind, but of course, doing so provides opportunities for measuring length, distance, height, area, mass, volume, and angles, and limitless circumstances to make basic through to advanced calculations. Among other organizations, the National Centre for Excellence in Teaching Mathematics has enthusiastically argued the case for teachers to make greater use of the outdoors in their lessons.[8]

---

8 See https://www.ncetm.org.uk/resources/9551

Physics and chemistry are important means of understanding, and to some extent predicting the processes that define our physical world. Some aspects of physics, such as observations of weather and climate, astronomy/cosmology, are obvious candidates.[9] A simple walk can provide opportunities to construct experiments and discuss principles of matter and motion – mass and density of objects, gravity, balance, friction, momentum, collisions; energy flow (e.g. from the sun, human bodies), absorption, and reflection. Similarly, understanding of chemical processes can, for example, be developed through measurements of pH in rain, soil, and water, or comparative studies of pesticides and organic gardening in garden beds in the school grounds. The concrete, bricks, mortar, and metals in our schools and other structures are all formed by chemical processes. These can be described and investigations conducted on the effects of water, heat, and pressure in breaking them down.

An integrated science session on a river can be a means of developing understanding of the *relationship of the sciences* in a 'real world' situation. For example, this can include aspects of biology (e.g. river ecology, adaptation, physiology), along with measurements of oxygen levels in water samples and measurements of stream volume and velocity. In turn, human dependence on water and water bodies, and human modification of aquatic environments (e.g. bridges, wind turbines, pollution and water treatment), can provide an entry point to utilitarian approaches to water use, and to a discussion of relative values. This can, of course, be juxtaposed with water's universal cultural significance, in terms of aesthetic and recreational appeal. Such an approach reflects the way in which knowledge must be applied across a range of subject areas to gain depth and contextual understanding.

Studies of community planning and development and other aspects of social studies benefit considerably from direct experiences outside the school (see Chapter 7). For example, visits to local town centres or agricultural areas, community gardens, municipal agencies, and public facilities can all provide rich material for discussion and project development in class. The learning from these local spaces and organizations can lead to deeper understandings of civics, citizenship, social roles and norms, employment, and social equity, while developing a sense of place and identity. All of these possible outcomes involve learning that a child can contextualize as part of their lived experience (see also Chapter 4).

One great strength of outdoor learning is that it is possible to provide opportunities for planning, decision-making, and responsibility-taking that

---

9 See for example Kibble's (2010) creative outdoor teaching resource that helps students better understand the relationship between the Earth and the Sun through experimenting with shadows.

transforms student learning into a more active enterprise. These aspects of what is often an 'informal' personal and social education curriculum can be integrated with more formal curricular areas to provide stimulating integrated learning opportunities. For example, short journeys with or without maps of local areas where route-finding decisions are required can be used to develop knowledge of the local environment.

This approach finds support from 'progressive education' philosopher, John Dewey (1973), who argued that the onus was on educators to place their students in 'indeterminate situations' (p. 227) that necessitated critical and creative thinking, decision-making, and problem-solving to negotiate. In other words, Dewey believed that the educator's job was not to lead students 'down a road' but to place students at 'forks in the road', where they had to assess the benefits and pitfalls of certain courses of action, and then act on their decision. Dewey's concept of the indeterminate situation is strongly connected to the way experiences are structured for learners, as it implies that educators need to coordinate learning environments where the participant may take many different courses of action.

The indeterminate situation has much resonance with recent work on the concept of *executive function*. The term refers to 'high-level cognitive processes required to plan and direct activities, including task initiation and follow-through, working memory, sustained attention, performance monitoring, inhibition of impulses, and goal-directed persistence' (Dawson & Guare, 2010, p. vii). Opportunities to develop these lifelong skills can clearly be further enhanced by venturing outside the confines of the classroom into more complex contexts.

The potential curricular use of the outdoors is clearly considerable and by no means confined to the subject areas that we have discussed thus far. Carefully constructed outdoor learning experiences can demonstrate the relationships between many subject areas and disciplines that are simply not visible in class-room settings. Teachers of students at all ages and stages, and in most subject areas, can find inspiration and opportunities in the outdoors.[10] With a little creative thought, teachers can move beyond the delivering of de-contextualized parts of the curriculum towards the kind of integrated, interdisciplinary knowledge and understanding of the 'real world' that is so valuable in life beyond school.

---

10 The Danish-based, European Union funded, 'Outlines' project exists to help teachers and teachers-in-training bring all curricular areas outdoors. See http://www.outdoor education.dk/

CASE STUDY

Lakeview Middle School has a considerable portion of their educational aims founded on authentic learning across the curriculum. The garden project that they developed using a participative approach with students, staff, parents, and local businesses illustrates the rich learning that can be elicited by tackling a 'real world' project on a substantial scale. Being in a more rural area, the school has relatively large grounds. However, it was almost bare, except for the painted lines of the soccer pitch. Students voiced their concerns about this at a student council meeting. From there, a few enterprising teachers, the principal, some interested parents, a local landscape contractor, and three grade six students formed a committee to explore the ways in which the school grounds could be used as a meaningful part of student learning. A school-wide fundraising initiative was undertaken to raise money that would be matched by a government grant.

Before long, plans had emerged to develop a garden. The garden would incorporate flowers, trees, and shrubs to enhance the garden and grow food as well. An extensive list of jobs was created. First, the land had to be measured and surveyed. Second, all kinds of supplies needed to be ordered: wooden fencing, rich soil and compost, stones, and wood chips. Various classes were assigned jobs that would be done over the weeks to prepare the site for planting. Community volunteers, parents, students, and of course, the landscaping company, worked with the students as they built fences and raised beds, and made durable walkways around the garden. Several hot-house 'poly tunnels' were also constructed so that food could be grown throughout the winter.

Once the site was prepared, flowers, trees, and shrubs were planted. Then vegetables, fruit, and herbs were planted in the hot-houses and raised beds. As with the building phase, students were fully engaged with growing food and tending to the shrubs and plants. Although the physical part of the gardening takes place outdoors, much of the planning takes place indoors. In the classroom, instructions about planting and tending to carrots can be found and calculations about how many packets of tomato seeds to order can be made.

The science teachers capitalized on the wealth of opportunities to discuss and study curricular subjects such as photosynthesis and pests; the domestic science teacher had school produce to cook with; the art and language and drama teachers all found ways of using the garden and other outdoor experiences to stimulate creativity in their classes. While various teachers used the garden to different degrees, almost all of them reported that students were more easily engaged in lessons when they had come in from the garden; discipline problems had reduced dramatically.

Some of the harvested fruit and vegetables were used for school lunches and some were sold at their new weekly Friday afternoon market. The highlight of the market was the blackberry jam that had been made from existing bushes at the end of the school ground. A competition had been held to design a catchy label for the jam, and the winning design was replicated for each jar. With a business starting to grow, students made budgets to help them manage the money they were spending on supplies against the money they were making from selling their produce.

A project such as this one can cater to students of all abilities, across a range of disciplines.

Although the school in this example has access to considerable resources (if initially under-used), there are many without such assets at their disposal, and of course plans must be made accordingly. However, there is little inspiration to be found in a tarmac-covered playground and in such cases developing outdoor learning with the curriculum may well require an earlier progression from school-grounds to the local environment (see Chapter 4).

In all forms of outdoor learning planning, it is vital to use the environment in an authentic rather than contrived way, as this makes the learning appropriate to the context and can demonstrate the interconnected nature of many aspects of the school curriculum. This provides an opportunity to distinguish between what Smith (2000) refers to as *process* and *product* models of curriculum. Here, the emphasis is on the *process* of becoming self-reliant 'successful learners', rather than simply on the *product* orientation of learning aspects of knowledge that will be of instrumental value in higher education and employment. Clearly, both approaches to learning are necessary. However, if teachers focus on the *process* of learning when outside the classroom and encourage critical reasoning and reflection on these experiences, they will help their students develop the skills to become self-reliant and successful in learning throughout life.

As with life in the real world, outdoor learning is usually inherently interdisciplinary. Outdoor learning is a key way of integrating curricula that, depending on age and stage, are often traditionally taught as separate subject areas (e.g. geography, literature, ecology, and history). There are clear benefits in teaching aspects of these subject areas in an integrated fashion (both indoors or outdoors), as this reflects the interdisciplinary nature of the real world – the way we interact with each other and our planet.

GUIDELINES

- For schools, the curriculum is the totality of all that is planned for children throughout their school years. Through this planning, subtle messages are conveyed (deliberately or inadvertently) about the relationships between subjects, the relevance of learning environments (e.g. the outdoors), and both personal and cultural values.
- Outdoor learning can provide an action-context for the formal and informal curriculum, and can support physical, academic, personal, and social development.
- The opportunities for academic development outdoors are extensive. Although almost any subject area in the curriculum can be enhanced this way, many formal parts of the curriculum are ideally suited to learning outdoors. Additionally, the outdoors offers interdisciplinary learning opportunities in realistic contexts that are at once different and complementary to those available indoors.
- There should be no 'competition' between indoor and outdoor learning. Both may be necessary to maximize students' learning opportunities. 'Good pedagogy' is 'good pedagogy', wherever the teaching takes place.
- In addition to curricular benefits, time spent outdoors in green-spaces and gardens has been shown to improve classroom concentration, achievement, physical fitness, and general well-being.

Chapter 3

Education for sustainable development

CHAPTER AIMS

- Understand the concept of sustainable development and its implication that all life on Earth is inter-dependent and inextricably linked to the Earth's physical and biological systems.
- Become aware of the relationship between sustainable development and international and inter-generational environmental justice.
- Recognize how outdoor environmental education and education for sustainable development can help in understanding our planetary systems, encouraging awareness of the impact of our actions, and fostering a values-oriented approach to personal environmental decisions.
- Acquire a range of principles and approaches that can help in planning integrated environmental and sustainable development education lessons both inside and outside the classroom.

WHAT IS EDUCATION FOR SUSTAINABLE DEVELOPMENT ?

The concept of 'education for sustainable development' (ESD) rests first on an understanding of 'sustainable development' (SD). Although SD is one of the most commonly used, abused, and misconstrued terms in use around the globe, it has an underlying fundamental premise. This has as much to do with the concepts of society and justice as with the science of our Earth systems. Indeed, the term is often linked with other words to explicitly illustrate this (e.g. 'sustainable development and social justice'). The discussion of terminology that follows is far from esoteric; it illustrates both the difficulty societies and their education systems experience in embracing the concept, and the central importance of critical thinking and analysis in this area.

The concept of 'sustainable development' has clear environmental origins, and can be traced back to work done in the 1980s by the International Union for the Conservation of Nature (IUCN) and its *World Conservation Strategy* (IUCN, 1980). By 1987 the concept was in common use and the World Commission on Environment and Development (1987) sought to bring some clarity to its use by defining sustainable development as 'development that meets the needs of the present without compromising the ability of future generations to meet their own needs' (p. 43). That this definition is still widely used owes much to its clarity and human-centred message, which seems to allow 'development' to continue. It appeals to a sense of progress and improvement, and makes it an attractive concept for both policy-makers and our industrialized society.

Growing concern about human impact on the environment in general, and in turn, the impact on human communities (especially in areas vulnerable to climate change), led to the 1992 UN Conference on Environment and Development (UNCED) in Rio de Janeiro, Brazil (often called the 'Earth Summit'). The ensuing report, *Earth Summit 1992*, commonly referred to as 'the Rio Accord' (UNCED, 1992), was important for several reasons. By this time, climate change had become a major concern to many governments and individuals, and the conference was the first attempt by the international community to develop a universal, wide-ranging plan to address human impact on the planet. The report also emphasized the role of education, both throughout the document and in a dedicated chapter.

A flurry of major international conferences followed in Kyoto (Japan, 1997), Johannesburg (South Africa, 2002), Montreal (Canada, 2005), Copenhagen (Denmark, 2009), and Cancún (Mexico, 2010), with a growing emphasis on climate change mitigation, and on international and inter-generational social justice. It is plain to see the growing acceptance that, counter to the ambition explicit in the above definition of sustainable development, our activities are certainly 'compromising the ability of future generations to meet their own needs' and, indeed, the *present* ability of some parts of the world to do so.

A generation has passed since the Earth Summit, and its exhortation to national governments that they should develop 'local' approaches. Most nations have published their own strategies concerning the interrelated issues of human-induced climate change, loss of biodiversity, and impacts on sustainable development and social justice. While much of the debate necessarily focuses on technical and scientific aspects (see for example, reports of the Intergovernmental Panel on Climate Change (IPCC)), many policy initiatives re-echo the significance of sustainable development education identified at Rio de Janeiro (Smyth, 1999).

This comprehensive approach, which argued that 'education should deal with the dynamics of both the physical, biological and socio-economic environment and human (which may include spiritual) development . . . and should employ formal and non-formal methods' (UNCED, 1992, p. 221), provides a rationale for outdoor as well as indoor learning, and indicates the significance of both content (curriculum) and approach (pedagogy) to sustainable development. This is clearly advocacy for education 'in, through and about' the outdoors (Lucas, 1979). This essentially rational approach has left many educators arguing that an emotional/affective element is essential in encouraging students to care for the future of all life on Earth.[1] Others have further argued that the outdoors is of central significance in providing opportunities, whereby all these elements of 'education for sustainable development' can be meaningfully integrated (Martin, 2008; Higgins, 2009; 2010).

The origin of the notion of 'education for sustainable development' and the statement made at the 1992 Earth Summit lie with the concept of 'environmental education', which was the focus of several intergovernmental conferences in the 1970s. The arguments and intent of these were clarified and developed at the 1977 Intergovernmental Conference on Environmental Education in Tbilisi, Georgia. The proceedings made clear and emphatic recommendations to governments on the key role of environmental education in sustaining our global environment, and published principles and guidelines for doing so.[2]

As with 'sustainable development', the concept of 'education for sustainable development' and its common synonyms is much debated. Perhaps the most widespread is the UNESCO definition:

> Education for sustainable development aims to help people to develop the attitudes, skills and knowledge to make informed decisions for the benefit of themselves and others, now and in the future, and to act upon these decisions.
>
> (UNESCO, 2010, para 3)

1 See Geddes' evocation of '*Heart, Hand and Head*' elaborated in Higgins and Nicol (2011); and Sobel's (2008) *Childhood and nature*.
2 For details see www.gdrc.org/uem/ee/tbilisi.html

The merits of the emphasis on solely human benefits, however, has been contested by some authors who take the stance that the Earth and its whole biological community need to be respected for more than their instrumental worth. It is a philosophical position that locates human beings within an interdependent ecological network whereby, if we significantly harm the network, we will harm our own species (see for example Leopold, 1966; Naess, 1989; Suzuki, 1997).

From this basic introduction it will be clear that universally accepted definitions of sustainability, sustainable development, and education for sustainable development are elusive. We have adopted the concept that 'sustainability' is more a direction of travel than a definition. As outlined in *The Earth Charter* (Earth Charter Initiative, 2000), this direction should focus on developing a 'global society founded on respect for nature, universal human rights, economic justice, and a culture of peace'. This way, 'education for sustainable development' can be viewed simply as education that aids us on our journey towards sustainability.

WHY IS EDUCATION FOR SUSTAINABLE DEVELOPMENT IMPORTANT?

Developing an understanding of the global implications of our daily actions is conceptually challenging, and all the more so when extrapolated into a future that can only be predicted by models, which are by their nature imprecise. Matters are further complicated by the influence of globalized economies, marketing, media, and politics – many facets of which inadvertently promote unsustainable behaviours. This situation offers both challenges and opportunities for the teacher.

Many current national and international sustainable development policies rely on the concept of 'societal choice'. Although these choices are complex and often confusing, they must be considered in any debate on human responses to an environmental issue. Their importance, and the role that levels of awareness and education play in informing such choices, cannot be overstated when it comes to successfully implementing any policy (sustainability-focused or otherwise). Education occupies a delicate position with regard to developing such behaviours. While educators cannot coerce their students to adopt certain behaviours, they play a key role in helping young people develop informed values to allow them to make personal choices. Although, in this context, many authors have contested the use of 'for' in the term 'education for sustainable development' and argued about its explicit 'values' stance, it is our view that on both pragmatic grounds (see IPCC reports) and philosophical grounds (e.g.

it embodies the notion of social justice), education must be *for* sustainable development.

Sterling (2001), amongst others, takes the view that sustainable development is of such central significance that schools should orient their structures and curriculum to deal with it: an approach he calls 'sustainable education'. His argument is that, as most of current educational provision is instrumental (developing skills for an industrial/commercial society), it takes little account of the 'increasing complexity, interdependence, and systems breakdown in the world' (p. 1).

As the evidence strongly suggests (IPCC, 2007) that this 'systems breakdown' is occurring, there seems little point in further arguing that education for sustainable development is of crucial importance. What is perhaps more worrying is that there are few signs of an imminent transformation of our current educational approach in order to address this. In this context, individual educators concerned with sustainable development will have to work pragmatically and urgently within current educational structures. This work rests on helping students make personal decisions on the basis of a clear understanding of Earth systems and ecological principles, and with an ethic of inter*national* and inter-*generational* justice.

The question then becomes, why is *outdoor learning* important in education for sustainable development? The most obvious reason is that it offers direct physical/sensory, intellectual, and affective ways of knowing the planet we depend upon for survival, and developing our relationship with it (see also Chapters 4 and 5). However, sustainability is a complex issue and much of both its conceptual difficulty and beauty lies in the relationships between parts of our planetary systems and the ways in which we interact with these. While outdoor learning cannot provide a comprehensive understanding, it can play a vital part in developing the broad understanding and relationships young people will need to move towards a more sustainable future.

In our evolution as a species, as well as our individual development from birth, we first came to know the world through physical/sensory experiences. Our senses provide the fundamental basis for a very personal way of *knowing* the world and experiencing the physical (landscape, geology, climate, weather) and biological world. Although these 'lived experiences' are fundamentally individual, they provide the basis of a common sensory understanding of our planet and an intellectual understanding of how it functions. Clearly, engaging with the natural world (outdoors) is central to this 'knowing', and perhaps even a necessary precursor of the critical reasoning skills and personal decision-making necessary for sustainable development. As Sobel (2008) notes, a bottom-up approach to sustainability involves direct experience and interaction – 'Talking to trees and hiding in trees precedes saving trees' – and he suggests that as educators we should be interested 'in figuring out how to cultivate relationships between children and trees in their own backyards' (p. 19).

An *intellectual* understanding of the environment through 'field studies' is a long-established outdoor learning tradition and continues to make an important contribution to education for sustainable development. Being able to see a geophysical or biological process, develop an understanding of form and function, and then potentially collect and analyze data offers a means of understanding that process. Significantly, all of this is training in the scientific method. While not confined to the natural sciences, the scientific method is a unifying principle that helps us to understand the world, and indeed, our capacity to modify and thrive in it. As our scientific knowledge has developed, it has been applied to bring many advances that benefit society (e.g. in medicine and technology) and, arguably, some that do not.

While a sense of wonder at the natural world does not solely rest on scientific understanding, there is also an inherent elegance and beauty in basic scientific laws and principles,[3] as well as in the complexity of our planetary systems. Without some understanding of these, we are at risk of failing to appreciate our complete dependence on our home planet. Furthermore, we are inclined to misjudge the consequences of both our own actions and important predictions, such as those relating to global climate change. It is also the scientific method, however, that allows us to examine the quality of the science and to interrogate and judge the ways in which politicians, the media, and the general public interpret (or misinterpret) the evidence for, and effectiveness of, our actions towards sustainable development.

The feelings or emotions we experience, when thinking about the planet and our relationship with it, will influence our actions in relation to sustainable development. This *affective* appreciation of our planet largely depends on direct personal, aesthetic, and even spiritual experience of it. While there are many ways in which such experiences can be enhanced or developed (through prose, poetry, art, music, and media), the basis of such an appreciation must involve sensory experiences and these are richest in outdoor environments.

One of the defining features of education for sustainable development is its *interdisciplinary* nature. While much can be learned from the careful examination of many individual facets of sustainability, complex interactions require specific attention to the 'whole' as well as the 'parts'. This requires an

---

3 For example, the importance of gathering and analysing empirical evidence; what constitutes a 'fair test' in an experiment; that 'being wrong' is just part of working towards a better understanding; that science is about uncertainty – while theories and models are about using good evidence to making the best predictions these can't be expected to be 'right'.

educator to focus on the environmental and social *systems* that characterize sustainable development. So, for example, the study of plants and animals, and the relationships between them (e.g. food webs), has a broader relevance when considering their role in the planetary flow of energy and cycling of nutrients. In turn, human impact on these systems has implications for global climate change: for example, water availability, agriculture, poverty, and social conflict. Such subject matter offers limitless opportunities for integrated classroom and outdoor learning through a wide range of 'ways of knowing'.[4]

Modern society is more urbanized than ever before; thus there is an increasing tendency for children to have ever more limited exposure to the natural world (Louv, 2008). This potentially adds to our future societal difficulties in relation to sustainable development, as there is a growing body of evidence that early experiences (Palmer & Suggate, 1996; Chawla, 1998) are significant in developing an ethic of care for the environment. If young people are not experiencing the natural world independently or in the company of family or friends, the role of guided outdoor experiences becomes increasingly significant.

HOW CAN TEACHERS INCORPORATE EDUCATION FOR SUSTAINABLE DEVELOPMENT INTO THEIR PLANNING?

Sustainable development appears in parts of many curricula, but is rarely a central focus. This happens despite it being a concept that, to be properly understood, demands an integrated, interdisciplinary approach. This requirement allows teachers to capitalize on the advantages of learning both inside and outside the classroom, with appropriate locations being chosen to enable the students' learning to be most effective.

So, for example, the global cycling of carbon and its relevance to climate change and global social equity are parts of curricula and quite appropriately taught in the classroom. However, linking this with appropriate multi-dimensional outdoor learning opportunities provides additional context, stimuli, and integration. The following case study offers one example of this approach – in this case study, carbon cycling and climate change.

---

4 See below and Gardner's (1993) theory of multiple intelligences

CASE STUDY: 'BY LEAVES WE LIVE'

Fraser often starts lessons with his grade 5 class with answers, to which the students must offer a 'question'. On this day, that answer is 'four minutes'. A range of suggested questions come forth from the class, but don't hit the mark. Fraser prompts them with the suggestion: 'If you hold your breath while you think, it will help you to concentrate.' When the right answer is called out ('If we are deprived of air, how long before we die?'), the successful student is rewarded with a small plant (usually a 'weed' from around the campus) in a newspaper pot. The reason for this is not explained at the time, and more indoor exercises on the 'elements' of life follow.

Moving outdoors, the students are then encouraged to observe plants (grass, 'weeds', trees, and so on) that may be growing around the campus and to discuss the green pigment of chlorophyll that allows the plants to photosynthesize (this is explicitly linked to classroom-based work). This theme is developed by considering the global significance of plants (such as the weed in the newspaper pot) in:

- absorbing carbon dioxide (CO_2) that we (and other animals) breathe out and which we produce through burning fossil fuels, and so on; and releasing oxygen that we and other organisms need to breathe;
- that their structure in the form of glucose and cellulose provides food for ourselves and other animals, and many other materials we depend on.

The students are then invited to help build a small fire with local twigs and sticks, and are asked to saw through some smaller logs. In doing so they are invited to look at the growth rings and to think of the human lifespan and history alongside that of a tree. (Depending on climate and tree species, even a 10cm diameter log may be older than the students.) The wood is then burned to illustrate how long it takes to grow and how quickly it is 'gone'. The process of building carbon into the structure of the wood and then its release (primarily as CO_2) is then discussed in the context of the global circulation of air masses (where do these atoms of carbon go and what becomes of them?) and extended to our use of fossil fuels (what formed them and what happens when we burn them?). The use of a geological timeline emphasizes the vast timescales (60 million years – from 360 to 300 million years ago) over which our oil reserves were laid down, and this is contrasted with the 200 years or so over which we have all but used these up (see Higgins, 2010).

Where possible, students are then given the chance to plant a tree (preferably) or some other plant, in order to reinforce some of the points made earlier. This is extended to ensure that we remember that the global loss of forests is not just a contemporary issue in places like the tropics; we in the developed countries have, of course, felled trees over many thousands of years. The fact that the carbon (and other elements) in these are also globally cycled, and have been ever since trees evolved, is also highlighted. A number of creative exercises and approaches are used to develop all these themes, which include published prose and poetry (see Higgins, 2010, for examples), and provide students with opportunities for creative writing.

While this exercise is delivered to teachers, it is designed for young people. The session can finish in a number of ways, highlighting, for example, other greenhouse gases (e.g. nitrogen oxides and methane relating to agricultural production), global food security, the consequences of population growth, loss of biodiversity, international, and inter-generational issues.

Although this case study offers a way of teaching the carbon cycle and related issues, it can also be used to emphasize the fundamental processes that sustain life on Earth and the importance of interdisciplinary studies to understand them. Depending on the age and stage of their students, teachers may consider stimulating their students to ask why, if these fundamental processes are so important, they are not a dominant feature of educational and governmental policy. This 'critical reasoning' is what takes the issue into the sort of values discussion that is essential if we are to help students envision and work towards a sustainable future. A teaching approach like the one in the case study brings students into contact with wood and plants, and if the location is chosen well, will provide direct exposure.

Sustainable development is clearly the most pressing and the most problematic of contemporary issues, and according to expert opinion will have to be addressed on a timescale of the next 10 to 50 years. As Tremmel, Page, and Ott (2009) remind us, 'Each generation has the duty not to engage in the wishful thinking that the problem can be left for descendants to solve' (p. 87).

Progress towards sustainable development is problematic as it requires major changes in the policies of governments and in our daily personal decisions. In order to move towards a sustainable future, students need to develop the critical thinking skills necessary to critique and challenge themselves, their politicians, and others with influence, over what is and what is not valued and promoted within society. This approach is supported by Tilbury and Wortman's (2004) view that the following skills should provide a structure for education for sustainable development:

- envisioning: being able to imagine a better future;
- critical thinking and reflection;
- systemic thinking: acknowledging complexities, looking for links and synergies in trying to find solutions to problems;
- building partnerships: promoting dialogue and negotiation, learning to work collaboratively;
- participation in decision-making.

To help students develop these skills, teachers need first to ensure that the selection of skills and the depth to which they are pursued are age and stage appropriate. They can then capitalize on the curricular relevance of the subject matter and take advantage of learning both inside and outside the classroom. The processes of building partnerships and participating in decision-making will require carefully constructed learning opportunities in the school (e.g. through an energy-saving campaign) and outside (e.g. negotiating with a landowner to plant trees). The strength of this approach lies in the locations being chosen to enable student learning to be most effective in helping them find meaning and personal relevance, and in developing the interdisciplinary understanding and skills necessary to address the issue of sustainable development.

GUIDELINES

- All species on Earth, including our own, are inescapably dependent on and are a part of global geophysical and ecological systems, and all our futures depend on the balance in these systems being maintained. If we significantly harm these systems, we harm our own species too, and educators must make developing such understanding a priority in their work.
- Education for sustainable development is ideally suited to an integrated mixture of indoor and outdoor interdisciplinary learning experiences close to the school environment.
- Outdoor learning has a key role in educating young people *about* our planet (environmental education) and *for* sustainable development.

- Carefully designed and delivered direct, multi-sensory outdoor learning experiences can encourage the development of a strong affective relationship with the natural world, and help young people understand the local, international and inter-generational consequences of their actions. In some cases this may well predispose the student to take action 'for' the environment.

Chapter 4

Learning through local landscapes

CHAPTER AIMS

- Understand that place-based education is all about 'where we are' – learning more about a place and coming to understand our own personal connections to it.
- Recognize that all landscape has a 'story', that this story can be socio-cultural or ecological, and that this presents an excellent unifying approach for learning outdoors.
- Appreciate how understanding local landscapes can involve students in learning about events that took places millions of years ago, or becoming involved in current land use issues.

WHAT IS LEARNING THROUGH LOCAL LANDSCAPES?

The importance of place-based learning has been highlighted by commentators in mainstream education and those from the outdoor learning sector. In the first decade of the millenium, an increasing number of educational critics have placed a growing emphasis on learning that focuses on local landscape (see, for example, Nicol & Higgins, 1998; Brookes, 2002; Smith, 2002; Stewart, 2004; Baker, 2005; Harrison, 2010). While this trend does not deny the value of grade 5 students from Alaska learning about the Brazilian rainforest, it may question why many of these young people are not first learning about the woods in their own neighbourhood. Furthermore, as the last chapter on sustainability highlighted, children may better understand issues relating to the Brazilian rain forest if they can contextualize them through direct experiences of their own local woodland.

Outdoor learning critics have noted that some traditional outdoor education programmes focus on developing intra- and inter-personal growth, and are so concentrated on the thrills and skills inherent in the activity that they ignore the 'story' of the land.[1] This kind of learning that takes place outdoors, but pays little attention to place, is called 'universal', as the activities can take place just about anywhere. Australian outdoor educator, Andrew Brookes (2002) is especially critical of outdoor programmes that treat landscapes 'as empty sites on which to establish social or psychological projects' (p. 405). This body of critical literature challenges educators to base their programmes on the locations in which they take place – not in what Baker (2005) has labelled 'Anywoods, USA'.

Higgins (2009) argues that developing a connection with place 'provides a start point for relationships (connections) with people within a community that allows further developmental outcomes, such as understanding the consequences of one's actions and an ethic of citizenship and care' (p. 48). He explains that many outdoor adventure education programmes take place far away from participants' homes. Within programmes such as these, 'building a lasting sense of connection in participants may be difficult to achieve as they develop relationships with a place other than their own place and perhaps with people they may never see again' (p. 48). These programmes that take place far from participants' home communities are often justified by their experiential approach and further predicated on the assumption that participants will be able to transfer their learning to life back home. This is a noble goal, but one that is very difficult to prove. In learning outside the classroom, a key aspiration is for learning contexts to be as authentic and connected to participants' 'real world' as possible. Indeed, place-based education aims to 'ground learning in local phenomena and students' lived experience' (Smith, 2002, p. 586). In addition, educational programmes that take place in the local landscape allow participants to continue their relationship with that place long after the formal schooling element has finished.

An educational model valuing local and place-based learning will have much of its content based on aspects of life that may be familiar, but not necessarily

1 See Beames (2006) for an overview of these critiques.

understood. Examples of this content could include finding out what the school grounds were used for before the school existed; looking into what kind of rock and soil lies under the school building and playground; and what birds, animals, trees, fungi, and plants are on the property – and why. This kind of approach is inherently cross-curricular; indeed, as Smith and Sobel (2010) tell us, 'Place can be drawn upon to teach any subject area' (p. 23). Focusing on place can lead to connections being made between subject areas.

Learning with an emphasis on place is closely linked to principles of community-based education. Smith and Sobel's (2010) book showcases how these two approaches are often intertwined in complex ways. We regard that having students come to know 'their places' is the starting point for most meaningful learning. From this point, educators can choose different ways to engage a) with the people who live and work in the local neighbourhood and b) with the landscape itself. Reflecting these emphases, Chapter 7 concentrates on community-based education, while the present chapter focuses on learning through the local landscape. Of course, these two areas are not mutually exclusive and will overlap to varying degrees, depending on the circumstances.

WHY IS LEARNING THROUGH LOCAL LANDSCAPES IMPORTANT?

Perhaps the primary underlying assumption behind place-based education is that directly interacting with 'place' will foster an appreciation of, and a broad ethic of caring for, the land and its varied inhabitants. Seen this way, schooling has more relevance to children's everyday lives, as it is rooted within a location that is familiar to them; it is learning that is 'situated'. This situated perspective recognizes the importance of the 'physical, social, and cultural environment on individuals' meanings, actions, development, and learning' (Rovegno, 2006, p. 271): children's attitudes, knowledge, and skills are heavily influenced by their interactions with other students, the academic curriculum, and the myriad external stimuli to which they are exposed.

Quite apart from the educational reasons that teachers might focus on learning through local landscapes, there is also one practical reason: if outdoor learning is something that can happen at any time during the school day (because the class can quickly travel to a given place on foot), it is more likely to take place on a regular basis than a trip that involves booking buses and travelling to somewhere further away from the school.

We suggest that the principal reason for incorporating a place-based learning programme in the school neighbourhood should not simply be one of convenience; learning and playing with one's people and in one's place has the capacity to firmly build an individual's sense of who one is. Percy-Smith and Malone (2001) explain that 'the value of local place experiences for children goes beyond issues of place, use and provision, yielding also potential opportunities for developing a sense of belonging, identity, self-worth and advocacy as fellow citizens within neighbourhood communities' (p. 18).

Canadian outdoor educator Bob Henderson frequently uses the term 'story' when discussing ways of knowing. Henderson moves our understanding away from a more one-dimensional conception of learning about the land's story to one that equally values 'story-making'. Drawing on work by Yi Fu Tuan, Henderson (2010) explains how space and place are not the same: 'space is unstoried place' (p. 84). Seen in this light, teachers and students become 'storiers', as they use places as sites through which to develop their 'agency, belonging, and competence' (p. 84). The word 'belonging' is important here. Through belonging to place – their place – they are not just story-learning and story-making, but *place-learning* and *place-making* (Henderson, 2010, p. 84).

HOW CAN TEACHERS INCORPORATE TEACHING THROUGH LOCAL LANDSCAPES INTO THEIR PLANNING?

In terms of the learning contexts outlined in the first chapter, local and place-based learning has strong and obvious links to the first two of four zones: the school grounds and local neighbourhood.

By now, you will understand that place-based education is all about 'where we are' – learning more about this place and coming to understand our own personal connections to this place. Following this logic, place-based education is equally important on day-long field-trips, overnight stays at residential outdoor centres, and multi-day expeditions.

When preparing teaching sessions that are place-responsive (e.g. that are rooted in local phenomena), it is important to keep in mind that there is not one 'right way' to do things. Smith (2002) notes that 'because place-based education is by its nature specific to particular locales, generic curricular models are inappropriate' (p. 587). The most appropriate approach to place-based learning is for the content to be uniquely suited to the surroundings. So, while an approach to learning and teaching may be employed in different landscapes and cultures (e.g. Metasaga,[2] Outdoor Journeys[3]), the content will be particular for each class, as the socio-cultural and ecological story of the

2 See http://metasaga.wikispaces.com/
3 See www.outdoorjourneys.org.uk

school grounds and surrounding area is going to be different for different schools – irrespective of whether they are 10 or 10,000 miles away from each other.

It is worth emphasizing that students in highly urbanized areas are just as able to learn about ecology as their counterparts who live in the country. Even in big cities there are infinite opportunities to learn that other living things (be they trees, moss, or squirrels) exist within surroundings that at first might seem quite unnatural. Inevitably, learning about the natural world forces us to consider how humans have influenced the way in which other living beings experience the place shared by all. Thus, even nature studies can involve learning about people and human-made objects as well as the non-human entities living in the same neighbourhood. It is perhaps common knowledge to an adult that the human and natural worlds are inextricably intertwined, but this may not be obvious to every 11-year-old.

A more engaging approach than simply learning facts about a given place can involve conserving or maintaining it. This might involve weeding, cleaning, picking up rubbish, painting, pruning, and so on. In this approach, the notion of taking pride in the care and upkeep of a particular place takes dominance. Naturally, having the young people decide on how they might care for 'their place' will almost certainly yield a more engaging and meaningful programme than one based on what has been deemed important by an adult. This will involve ensuring that students have sufficient power to allow curiosity to drive their learning, as well as their capacity to be responsible people, to manage that learning.

Students often take great interest in growing food that can be used for their own consumption. Indeed, there are examples of schools that have grown food and then sold it as part of an enterprise project that involved running a small business.[4] In conservation and growing projects there is much scope for using and managing equipment and tools, and for developing landscaping and building skills (e.g. constructing raised beds or poly-tunnels). Certainly, using student curiosity as a starting point can be especially effective in allowing the content to be more relevant to students' personal interests (see Chapter 5).

4 Visit Scotland's Rothesay Academy 'Young Green Fingers' website for more information. http://www.rothesayacademy.org.uk/pages/about-the-school/young-green-
   fingers.php

LANDFULNESS

Molly Baker's (2005) *landfulness* framework is a helpful means of enabling students to bring meaning to place. The name is a play on Aldo Leopold's (1966) lament that we are a people 'among whom education and culture have become almost synonymous with landlessness' (p. 210). Baker proposes a model with four stages:

1   Become deeply aware of our place in the landscape, on the map. What is around us?
2   Understand what has happened to shape this place – environmentally, culturally, historically. What was this place like 100 years ago?
3   Become aware of what happens in this place now. Who uses it? Whose habitat is this?
4   Connect with the place once you go home. How can we remain mindful of this place, once at home?

Although Baker's framework suggests that it may have been created to assist students as they get to know a place that they are visiting, which is 'away' from their local neighbourhood (note the phrase 'when you go home'), it is just as applicable for young people who are learning about their 'home turf'.

We regularly use Baker's four-step approach when working with student teachers. Often the simplest framework, like this one – or the Questioning, Researching, and Sharing one from Outdoor Journeys (see the case study on page 53) – can provide teachers and students with just enough structure to organize a self-directed programme of learning.

CASE STUDY

In a nearby urban park, Ben runs landfulness sessions for his 24 grade 3–4 students. Inspired by Baker's (2005) four steps, he begins by handing groups of two or three students a *ziplock* bag that includes a sheet of A3 paper and some crayons.

Each group is instructed to become deeply aware of what is around them. This involves drawing their own map of their surroundings (perhaps only using one quarter of their sheet of A3). To this map, students will then add labels for everything they know (e.g. street names, buildings, trees). Once this is completed, students will write down questions about everything they don't know. Some examples of this might include the names of trees, how long buildings have existed, and the origins of a statue. Already, the blank sheet is getting crowded: the landscape is coming alive.

The next step is to look at what has shaped this place throughout history. Ben uses a simple timeline on a path. Students are placed in twos or threes at various intervals. The first — as far away on the path that people can hear — is, unsurprisingly, the origins of our planet, some 4.6 billion years ago. After adding in the last eruption of a nearby volcano (350 million years ago), the dinosaurs' extinction (60 million years ago), the appearance of early humans (*Homo erectus*) (200,000 years ago), and the last ice age (11,000 years ago), we can start to focus on more local history such as the first signs of humans in this area, the first settlements, the first signs of industry, and when the park became an official park. Through this activity, students come to understand how the land has not always looked like it does now, but rather has been shaped by geomorphological processes over billions of years, and more recently by the actions of humans.

The third step involves using two activities to highlight the tensions inherent in current use of the land. The first activity starts with participants standing in a circle. Ben then reads out a series of statements that have to do with park use, such as: smoking should be banned, a cafe should be opened, bicycles should be banned, security cameras should be installed, large parts of the park should be closed to humans, and so on. Those who agree with the statements take a step forwards and those who disagree take a step backwards. Although people are generally influenced by their peers, a series of relatively rapid statements can address this to a degree. The point of the exercise is to show that different people have differing ideas about how public green spaces need to be used and managed.

The second activity that relates to Baker's third step of 'What is happening here now' is a role-play exercise. Ben begins by asking each person in the class to think of one particular user of the park. Typical answers include: joggers, nature-lovers, parents with baby strollers, teenagers drinking alcohol, dog-walkers, dogs, rabbits, and so on. As the students go around in the circle, it becomes harder to think of something that hasn't been suggested! Participants are then asked to enthusiastically take on the identity of the human (or animal) they have shared with the group and to interact with as many other 'park users' (members of the group) as possible. For two minutes, the class should have some fun, close interaction in their roles of park users. As with the last activity (statement agreement and disagreement), this different park-users activity quickly demonstrates that many others regard this shared landscape very differently from the ways that we do.

The final step is connecting this landfulness exercise to home. Through discussion at the end of the session and homework, students are encouraged to re-examine their home town (or current 'place') by learning about its story.

It should be noted that the A3 map is revisited throughout this session. Therefore at the end of the session, each group has a self-constructed map of the area that has labels, facts, and questions to be researched. Indeed, each student is asked to generate a question about the landscape before they leave the session. This way at the beginning of the next class, 24 new nuggets of highly varied, personally relevant knowledge will be shared with fellow students. The communal 'pot' of knowledge about this place has grown.

Meaningful learning outside the classroom does not require students to be bussed to far away locations and to take part in adrenaline-raising activities run by specially-trained instructors. On the contrary, cross-curricular, place-based educational initiatives that involve students taking responsibility for planning and undertaking journeys from their school grounds can be a crucial way of learning about socio-cultural and ecological elements of the local landscape. Lastly, learning about, caring for, and developing love for, a place takes time; repeated visits and long-term projects can help build meaningful and lasting relationships between people and their places.

GUIDELINES

- Learning through local landscape can enable students to develop meaningful connections with their peers, their people, and their place.
- Developing these connections can be facilitated by students seeing the consequences of their actions towards the land and other people.
- 'Place-making' involves more than just learning about the human and physical geography of a place; it demands that students (who are of course community members) actively construct the ongoing story of a place.

Chapter 5

Harnessing student curiosity

CHAPTER AIMS

- Explore theoretical ideas that focus on child development and the importance of curiosity as an organizing principle for learning.
- Understand the roles of learners and teachers in nurturing curiosity.
- Investigate special opportunities for fostering curiosity in the outdoors.

WHAT IS CURIOSITY?

What is it that prompts us to do something and not something else, and what provides the stimulus for doing anything in the first place? A variety of different theories of motivation explain how human behaviour is driven by unsatisfied needs. One obvious example is the biological drive to survive. However, beyond the essential need to survive, humans are naturally driven to make sense of the world around them. For this to happen, human motivation must transcend instrumental survival needs and include the psychological domain (Atkinson, Smith, Bem, & Hoeksema, 1993). There is one key motive that stimulates a desire in us to actively explore our physical surroundings: the essential nature of this motivation is what we call 'curiosity'.

Look in any dictionary and you will find the word 'curiosity' described along the lines of a desire to know and learn. Furthermore, the curious mind is often referred to as inquisitive and stimulated by active learning methods such as exploration, adventure, creativity, discovery, investigation, and observation. Curiosity is everywhere in our social world. It inspires our scientists to greater discoveries, our philosophers to keep asking deeper questions, our teachers to teach, and learners to learn. In our everyday lives it influences our choice of holidays, whom we choose to socialize with, what products we buy in the shops, and so on. It is so much a part of our lives that it is easy to overlook and take for granted. However, curiosity is central to stimulating the mind and it is important to remember that a major purpose of the brain is to learn.

Despite being such a common word (and perhaps because of this reason) scholars are not always in agreement about how to define curiosity. In academic literature, Maw and Maw (1970) have stated that the child can be said to be curious when he or she

> (a) reacts positively to new, strange, incongruous, or mysterious elements in his [sic] environment by moving towards them, exploring them, or manipulating them; (b) exhibits a need or a desire to know more about himself [sic] and/or his [sic] environment; (c) scans his [sic] surroundings seeking new experiences; and/or (d) persists in examining and/or exploring stimuli in order to know more about them.
>
> (p. 124)

This definition begins to hint at why the outdoors offers more contrasting and varied learning opportunities than indoors. The 'journey' has been a corner-stone in the historical development of outdoor education and scientific exploration. While Maw and Maw (1970) provide a definition for curiosity as a concept, if you read it again they could easily be explaining the motivation for exploration and the experiences people have when they go outdoors. This blend of curiosity and the outdoors is something that we have come to call 'learning journeys'.

Curiosity remains an elusive concept until it is located with a body of theory, and much has been written about learning theory that shows how curiosity can be nurtured in an educational context. In 1943, Maslow (2010) developed a theory of human motivation where all human needs first depended on satisfying survival needs such as food, water, and shelter. His 'hierarchy of needs' argued that these 'lower order' (sometimes referred to as 'fundamental') needs had to be met before 'higher order' needs could be satisfied.

Maslow's hierarchy has been criticized because it suggests a linear progression; higher order needs further up the pyramid cannot be met until fundamental needs lower down have been satisfied. However, Wilber (2000) suggests that needs are in fact integral, rather than linear. In other words there are relationships between needs that are not necessarily hierarchical. An example helps to show the complexity of needs. Participation in high-risk adventure such as climbing Himalayan mountains shows how the need for 'love and belonging' can be de-prioritized (either consciously or unconsciously). This is because 'safety' (a more fundamental need) cannot be guaranteed and there is always a significant risk of not returning to loved ones. In this way 'safety' and 'love and belonging' are reversed, as the drive to climb mountains provides a stronger motivational need despite the possibility of injury and death. To complicate matters further, it is possible that if the climber does succeed they may return home to a 'hero's welcome' and may in fact experience 'self actualization' (the highest level of need) and then experience 'esteem needs' from an adoring public.

What does this mean for learning and teaching in the outdoors? The Swiss psychologist Jean Piaget (1977), despite being a biologist himself, stated, 'it would be unwise to rely on biological "nature" alone to ensure the dual progress of conscience and intelligence' (p. 392). Piaget was keen to explore the difference between 'nature' (behavioural traits that people are born with) and 'nurture' (the role of personal experience in the learning process). He conducted a range of experiments and found that children's learning is developmental because it is linked to their maturity. As such, their capacity to learn increases through childhood as they get older and more mature.

Another major figure in learning theory was the American Carl Rogers. He emphasized a 'person-centred approach' that placed the learner at the centre in order to celebrate their individual creativity and problem-solving abilities (1983). This is often referred to in modern curricular literature as 'differentiated learning', where the teacher is required to identify and work at the different intellectual levels of individuals within the same group (this idea is explored further in Chapter 6). For Rogers, the key to this approach was the learner being responsible for their own learning and the teachers facilitating this process. In terms of relevant content and methods it was important to consider not just what was taught but how it was taught. The classroom activities that Rogers had in mind would be characterized by a curriculum where children had some influence in the selection of what was to be learnt. Perhaps the most important tenet of Rogerian thinking is that the ultimate purpose of education is for learners to learn how to learn (Rogers, 1983).

Common to Piaget and Rogers was the recognition of the importance of experiential approaches to teaching and learning what Bee (1989) has referred to as 'active voluntary exploration' (p. 227). The two psychologists believed that self-initiated learning encourages a questioning approach that involves active enquiry, discovery, and problem-solving abilities. The success of this approach depends to a large extent on the willingness of the learner to engage in this process and it is here that curiosity has a major function. As Rogers (1983) says of children, 'it is their curiosity, their eagerness to learn, their ability to make difficult and complex choices that will decide the future of our world' (p. 1).

WHY IS CURIOSITY IMPORTANT?

Daniel Berlyne was a pioneer in the study of curiosity. He described curiosity as 'the brand of arousal that motivates the quest for knowledge and is relieved when knowledge is procured' (1960, p. 274). Day (1982) was a student of Berlyne's and extended his work by positing that a person's optimal level of curiosity is something that is characterized by their interest, excitement, and desire to explore. Below this optimal level, the individual will likely be unmotivated, disinterested, and inefficient, whereas being above it will yield defensive, disinterested, avoidance, and inefficient behaviours. Understanding the relationship between curiosity, arousal, knowledge, and procurement is central to learning and teaching.

The pioneering Russian psychologist, Lev Vygotsky, had much in common with his contemporary Piaget, in that they were both interested in how children learn. Where Piaget focused on the importance of the individual, Vygotsky (1978) emphasized the development of interpersonal relations. He stated that 'learning presupposes a specific social nature and a process by which children grow into the intellectual life of those around them' (p. 88). This suggests that individuals can flourish even more within a learning community than they can alone.

Vygotsky (1978) developed a concept known as the 'zone of proximal development' (ZPD), which offers a clear way of understanding how curiosity can be a key motivating factor in learning and teaching outdoors. He defines ZPD as 'the distance between the actual developmental level as determined by independent problem solving and the level of potential development as determined through problem solving under adult guidance or in collaboration with more capable peers' (p. 86). In other words, while 'children's solo performance is of interest . . . a child's optimum level is achieved when working jointly with a more knowledgeable person' (Schaffer, 2004, p. 200). The zone refers to the difference between the learner's intellectual and emotional starting points and their potential to learn more. This is where the boundaries of knowledge are progressively extended. Once the teacher identifies the developmental level of the child, this then becomes the starting point for the next teaching episode. In this way 'what a child can do with assistance today she will be able to do by herself tomorrow' (Vygotsky, 1978, p. 87).

We can see from this discussion that the call for person-centred learning does not imply a chaotic classroom (indoor or outdoor) with a minimal role for the teacher. The teacher has a pivotal role. Wood (1998) points out that 'children who are unable to perform tasks, solve problems, memorize things or recall experiences when they are left to their own devices often succeed when they are helped by an adult' (p. 26). This idea has been referred to as 'scaffolding', which is a metaphor designed to highlight the role of the teacher in support of student-centred learning. Scaffolding can be thought of as 'the wide range of activities through which the adult, or more expert peer, assists the learner to achieve goals which would otherwise be beyond them, for example by modelling an action, by suggesting a strategy for solving a problem or by structuring the learning into manageable parts' (Smith, Cowie, & Blades, 1998, p. 431).

The theory introduced so far provides guidance for the interaction between student and teacher. Learning implies a conscious effort on behalf of the learner. It is for teachers to help learners explore representations of their experience and what that experience means in a wider social and natural context. This is in keeping with Illich's (1996) position that education should be a balance between the personal choices of the student and mentoring by the teacher.

HOW CAN TEACHERS INCORPORATE CURIOSITY INTO THEIR PLANNING?

Having outlined some theoretical underpinnings of curiosity and how it can be nurtured through teaching and learning, it is important to discuss why curiosity should be taken outdoors. As human beings we respond to what is around us. If we are in a classroom, then the stimulus for curiosity is contextualized by an important factor – the physical space. The same can be said of the outdoors.

However, in comparing these physical spaces it is safe to say that they are very different, particularly in the way we experience them. Louv (2008) has stated that 'studies of children in schoolyards with both green areas and manufactured play areas found that children engaged in more creative forms of play in the green areas' (p. 88). Crucially, he points out that 'natural settings are essential for healthy child development because they stimulate all of the senses and integrate informal play with formal learning' (p. 86).

We should bear in mind that 'as soon as they [the children] are able to ask *questions*, they do so about the things that have aroused their curiosity' (Hurlock, 1978, p. 206). Willison and O'Regan (2007) note that learning 'is motivated by a need to know about, or a curiosity about, how things are, and what things do or may do' (p. 398). They go on to state that the pre-eminent

51

characteristic of curiosity and learning is simply to 'wonder why', and argue that children have this capacity at an early stage.

Many children, however, have very little experience of the outdoors. This 'disconnection' has important implications for all facets of children's learning, growth, and development (Louv, 2008, pp. 2–3). Apart from the genuine need for children to have greater exposure to the outdoors, from this perspective there is another dimension that needs to be asserted. This has to do with the joy of learning that is found when the powerful urges of curiosity combine with the equally powerful stimuli available outdoors. Willison and O'Regan (2007) view learning as a journey that is catalyzed by curiosity, and believe that education 'should lead them to ask research questions of increasing sophistication, specificity, depth and breadth, that set them on a journey towards making the unknown known' (pp. 398–399).

If we follow this logic, then the implication for teachers is to harness curiosity and use it as a means for students to effectively learn about the world they inhabit (outdoors as well as indoors). The recent *Learning outside the classroom* (CLOC, 2006) manifesto in the UK reflects this thinking. It states that 'research suggests the need to re-engage learners with the world as they actually experience it'. This is often called 'experiential' or 'authentic' learning. All of this clearly echoes Piaget (1977), Vygotsky (1978), and Rogers (1983). Here, therefore, is a modern document that supports outdoor learning and is underpinned by theory developed by some of the towering figures in child development and teaching and learning. The manifesto encourages outdoor learning by stating that 'young people are intensely curious and should be given the opportunity to explore the world around them' (CLOC, 2006, p. 3).

Arnone (2003) claims that instilling curiosity in students is really about encouraging their own innate disposition to learn. To this end, she suggests a number of teaching strategies that may arouse curiosity. We have adapted these to form four broad strategies, so that when a teacher takes their class outdoors, their reasons for doing so are to:

- provide and develop the physical space in the outdoors where curiosity can flourish;
- use curiosity eliciting elements such as incongruity, uncertainty, and conflict;
- foster an environment where enquiring, investigating, and questioning is the norm; and
- give students the power to direct substantial amounts of their learning.

We are at a point now where we can safely say that there is a world outside the classroom where curiosity and curriculum combine to offer powerful stimuli

52

for learning. Integrating outdoor and indoor teaching places the focus on arousing children's curiosity about landscapes and communities within the scope of their everyday lives.

CASE STUDY

Waverley Middle School wanted to look at ways of capitalizing on their students' interest in the local area. A group of keen teachers had heard about a simple approach called Outdoor Journeys, which would help them facilitate student-driven learning about the story of the local landscape.[1]

The idea was that by planning and undertaking local journeys, students would be able to learn across the curriculum in a manner that was personally relevant, experiential, holistic, and contextualized. The main focus of the approach involved students generating and answering questions about the socio-cultural and ecological story of the land. The teachers had read that Outdoor Journeys is structured into three phases that are negotiated, in terms of time and content, between the students and their classroom teacher. First, *Questioning* involves students exploring their school grounds and neighbourhoods and posing questions about the story of the land. Second, *Researching* enables groups of students to examine a topic of common interest (e.g. trees, architecture, maps, stone walls) through books, the Internet, or by interviewing people. Finally, *Sharing* involves students sharing what they have learned with their classmates and other members of the community, through writing, drama, video, photography, art, and music. These three phases can exist in a perpetual spiral, in that the learning can continue and develop through subsequent journeys. This approach also allows for progression of core skills within the three phrases in a meaningful and child-centred way.

The teachers hoped that throughout these journeys, their students would generate and answer questions about:

- *The human story of the land.* Who lived and/or worked here 50 years ago? 200 years ago? 2,000 years ago? How have they shaped the land? What is their story? Who owns the land? Who is 'using' the land and for what purposes?

1 See www.outdoorjourneys.org.uk

> • *The ecological story of the land.* What plants, flowers, trees, and moss are present? Why? What evidence of bugs, birds, can be found? Why have these living things chosen to live here, as opposed to somewhere else?
>
> After six weeks of doing Outdoor Journeys work, conversations with students at Waverley showed that they had learned much about the ecology, architecture, and history of the land within a kilometre of their school. Despite most of them living within walking distance of the school, many students were surprised by how little they previously knew of their neighbourhood's story.

Approaches like Outdoor Journeys are ideal for teachers, as they are already well schooled in the theories of child development. Teachers know about the emphasis that Vygotsky (1978) placed on nurturing social relationships in order to maximize learning. They also recognize the imperative for student-centred approaches, as Rogers (1983) and others have pointed out. Teachers are also aware of the importance that Piaget (1977) attached to age, stage, and maturity and are well equipped to differentiate learning accordingly.

Outdoor Journeys offers a wonderful opportunity for teachers to 'dip their toes' in the outdoors and discover for themselves how curiosity transforms learning in ways that theory alone cannot easily explain. This is not to denounce the importance of theory, but suggests that when the nurturing of curiosity becomes a central focus of learning, the outdoors provides an endless range of opportunities.

Central to this chapter has been the theme that teachers do not need specialist training to embark on learning journeys outdoors. Teachers already have a high degree of background knowledge in terms of teaching and learning. They also know the importance of curiosity in the learning process. When the curious mind is active, the learner can do a lot of the teacher's job by focusing on phenomena that interests them. This 'naturally occurring data' is different outdoors than indoors and the evidence we have presented shows the untapped curricular potential that awaits the curious teacher when they step outdoors.

We now know that an emphasis on indoor learning can lead to a suppression of the feelings from which respect, curiosity, wonder, and awe for the world beyond the classroom grow (Orr, 1992; 2004). This is a reminder of the importance of multi-sensory learning and how children's natural curiosity can be dulled by powerful audio-visual attractions such as video screens. The unpredictable quality of the outdoors stimulates exploration through curiosity, observation, testing, accepting or rejecting hypotheses, acquiring new knowledge, and theory building. This may sound grand and theoretical, but it is really a description of the way children (and adults for that matter) learn about the natural and social world around them. It is nothing less than the discipline of thought that is 'the scientific method', which is so valuable in developing critical thinking skills and values. This is not a challenge to indoor learning so much as an appraisal of what might be better learned out-of-doors. Our intention here is to encourage teachers to take their expert knowledge outdoors, confident that they have curiosity on their side.

GUIDELINES

- When children are given the opportunity to explore outdoor places, curiosity and curriculum combine to provide powerful stimuli for learning.
- Curiosity is central to student-centred learning and is a unifying theme that allows the teacher to complement indoor learning with outdoor learning.
- We need to be careful that modern lifestyles do not lead to the suppression of curiosity, and provide outdoor learning opportunities accordingly.
- School teachers are best placed to take learning outdoors because of their background training and specialist knowledge in how children learn best.
- Armed with the knowledge that children are naturally curious, teachers can be confident that when they take the curriculum outdoors, a new world of learning opportunities awaits.

Chapter 6

Enabling students to take responsibilities

CHAPTER AIMS

- Understand the roles of learners and teachers in nurturing responsible learners.
- Explore the special opportunities of doing so in the outdoors.
- Describe how this theme encourages transferable learning between the indoors and outdoors.
- Learn about using Personal Learning Plans for outdoor learning.

WHAT ENABLES STUDENTS TO TAKE RESPONSIBILITIES?

What is it that makes responsible learners? Are they the obedient ones who do what they are told? Do they always volunteer for jobs the teacher wants done? Scharle and Szabó (2000) remind us that students are not simply 'teacher's pets' who do things in order to please someone else in a position of power and authority.

So who is it that is responsible for learning? It would appear there are at least three answers to this question. It could be the teacher, the learner, or some combination of both. What is certain is that for learning to occur *someone* must take responsibility for it! One way to explore this is to consider the different ways that a teacher might perceive their role. For example, some teachers might ask themselves, 'What am I going to teach?', while another might ask, 'What do the students want (or need) to learn?'

Starting the discussion with the teacher does not imply that the teacher's role is more important than the learner's, only that it is a convenient starting point. Indeed, the semantics distinguishing the teacher from the learner are only problematic if one looks at one in isolation from the other. Therefore, we must turn to the *relationship* between teaching and learning in order to understand the different roles of each. As soon as the focus becomes relationships, the vast opportunities for learning begin to reveal themselves. As Wood (1998) observes,

> [teaching] both formal and informal, in many social contexts, performed by more knowledgeable peers or siblings, parents, grandparents, friends, acquaintances and teachers – is the main vehicle for the cultural transmission of knowledge.
>
> (p. 27)

It is important, though, that the role of the individual is not overlooked within this wider cultural context. Scharle and Szabó (2000) remind us that responsible learners are people who 'accept the idea that their own efforts are crucial to progress in learning, and behave accordingly' (p. 3). There are important conclusions to be drawn from these statements. First, the motivation for learning is not just something extrinsic (such as pleasing the teacher), but that crucially, children are intrinsically motivated to learn for themselves. Rogers (1961) suggests that for this to happen, individuals have to learn to trust themselves. He said this begins to happen when they have 'dared to feel their own feelings, live by values which they discover within, and express themselves in their own unique ways' (p. 175).

Here, then, is the rich learning potential identified when the zone of proximal development and scaffolding (outlined in the previous chapter) are practically applied. It follows that part of the teacher's responsibility is to create a collaborative learning community in which students can learn from each other, as well as from adults. This is a learning community that recognizes Piaget's (2002) evidence that individual differences in students' learning abilities are affected by age, developmental maturity, and gender. Reading this 'readiness to learn' that acknowledges 'age and stage' is a vital role of the teacher in enabling responsible learners. For this to happen, the process should include differentiation 'to suit the learning needs and prior learning of your students and to ensure that all are engaged in activities which challenge them

57

appropriately' (Dymoke & Harrison, 2008, p. 77). Differentiation allows for mixed ability, mixed age, mixed support, mixed resources, and mixed outcomes, and affects learning in groups as well as individuals (Glover & Law, 2002). As we will see, teachers who embrace the principles of differentiation are particularly well placed to capitalize on the outdoors as a multi-dimensional setting for learning.

Of the four outdoor learning contexts (referred to in Chapter 1), teachers working in the first two contexts (school grounds and local neighbourhood) are ideally placed to develop their practice, which is probably already very child-centred; the curriculum can easily be covered by building upon children's interests – a real bottom-up approach. The skill of the teacher is knowing the curriculum inside out and being creative and confident enough to respond to children's interests.

In summary, the key points here are:

- teaching and learning are characterized by a complex set of relationships;
- teaching and learning involves a wide peer group;
- the individual is at the centre of the learning process;
- learning also takes place beyond the classroom and includes other physical and social settings.

WHY IS TAKING RESPONSIBILITY FOR LEARNING IMPORTANT?

Responsibility for learning applies to both indoor and outdoor learning contexts. However, being outdoors provides different challenges and opportunities in which the responsible learner can flourish. Research into residential outdoor education in the UK noted that most programmes were short in duration, high in exciting activities, and were instructor intensive (Nicol, 2001). In terms of responsible learning, a crucial finding was that the chosen activities and the intended outcomes were, for the most part, instructor-led. This is clearly seen in Nicol's (2001) observation where everyday activities were 'less concerned with interpersonal processes and pupil-centredness and more by a didactic[1] relationship between instructor and pupil' (p. 226). Consequently, with few exceptions, students were allowed to take very little responsibility for their own learning.

---

1 In many parts of the world 'didactic' simply refers to the science of teaching and learning. However in the UK it has come to be used as a criticism of teaching that focuses on instruction at the expense of learner-centred approaches.

Table 6.1 Dimensions associated with narrow and broad conceptions of adventure

Narrow view of adventure	Broad view of adventure
Short timescale of experience	Long timescale of experience
High thrill challenges	Many challenges – varied in nature
Little or no effort involved	Some or much effort involved
No responsibilities devolved to students	Responsibilities devolved to students

Source: Rubens (1997, 1999)

Through a review of the literature on education and adventure and inter-views with experienced outdoor educators, teacher and outdoor practitioner Des Rubens (1997, 1999) provided evidence of important distinctions between what he calls 'narrow' and 'broad' adventure (see Table 6.1 above).

Higgins and Nicol (2002) have said of Rubens' work:

> he argued that the current literature on motivation in learning suggests the value of a 'mastery' approach to learning and contrasts 'narrow' and 'broad' views of adventure. 'Narrow adventure' experiences are in essence activities which are short in duration and focus on high thrills, but require little effort on the part of the student who takes minimal responsibility for his or her actions. In outdoor adventure activities zipwires, ropes courses and abseiling may be cited as examples. He contrasts this with 'broad adventure' which provides the converse, but most notably requires the student to take responsibility for their actions and sustain effort . . . Rubens . . . makes a strong case that 'broad adventure' . . . leads to a willingness in students to take responsibility for their actions in later life.
>
> (pp. 8–9)

Going outside in one's local neighbourhood may not seem as adventurous as taking part in adrenaline-raising outdoor activities, but what this research shows is that traditional notions of outdoor education can be limiting. The point here is that for a young child, exploring a local neighbourhood can offer a 'higher degree of authentic adventure than highly regulated ropes course and rock climbing sessions that are common at traditional residential outdoor centres' (Beames & Ross, 2010, p. 106). Furthermore, when the student steps outside the classroom it is easier for their teacher to have in mind the sorts of long-term curricular goals that involve the levels of effort and devolved responsibility for learning that are not possible in short-duration programmes. Schools are well

59

placed to nurture the sorts of long-term relationships between teachers and students that are necessary to nurture devolved responsibility.

It is not our intention to offer competing views of outdoor versus indoor learning. The outdoors is not offered here as a panacea for developing responsible learners, as we know that the theme of responsibility is already a feature of much class-based learning. However, there is evidence to suggest that the environment in which learning takes place (whether indoors or outdoors) has an effect on the way in which responsibility can be nurtured. In summarizing this research, Bilton (2010) concluded that 'the overwhelming sense is of children in a child-initiated activity, doing real work, of being very capable, motivated and engrossed. They are fantastic examples of quality outdoor activity' (p.153). We suggest that children can develop their responsibility for learning in an outdoor setting when the learning is:

- context specific (i.e. outdoors);
- intrinsic;
- consequential;
- clearly understood in terms of responsibility.

An example will help to explain these principles. If a teacher announces 'Children we are going outside – put your warm clothes and rain jackets on', just imagine some of the consequences. Once outside, one child might say 'my hands are cold' and blame the teacher by saying 'you never told me to take my gloves'. Although the learning episode was context specific (outdoors in the cold) it was not intrinsic, because the child did not take any personal responsibility. Furthermore, the child accepted no responsibility for its own actions and ended up blaming the consequences on the teacher. The relationship that was being nurtured here (whether consciously or unconsciously) was one of dependency.

Another way to specifically focus on responsibility in the same circumstances would be for the teacher to announce to the children 'We are going outside – what will we need to take with us to keep warm?' There might follow a question and answer session where an equipment list is written up for all to see and contribute to. Of course, the teacher can fill in any obvious omissions if they wish (although they may decide not to so that individuals can experience real consequences – within the bounds of safety, of course). With the planning complete, the children can collect the items they have agreed they need and proceed outdoors. It is then not so easy for the teacher to be blamed for any consequences when the decision-making was based on cooperative enquiry. Experiencing the consequences in this manner provides opportunities for the teacher to remind the student (if this is necessary) of their own roles in decision-making, and thereby reinforce the intrinsic aspects of learning.

It is important to note that while this situation describes an event in the outdoors, principles 2–4 (above) apply equally to the indoors and outdoors – with approaches such as developing responsible learners complementing one another. When carefully managed, there can be a reciprocal relationship that combines learning in the outdoor and indoor environment. What is different about the first principle, though, is that the outdoors can provide a stimulus that is immediate and direct. Reading about cold hands is very different from experiencing them; the consequences are direct and personal, and blaming someone else does not make them warm again! Examples such as these show how the outdoors can enhance active student responsibility in a way that the indoors cannot. Not only does the outdoors offer learning opportunities such as these, but they can be used as a way of generalizing beyond the immediate experience to thinking about responsibility for learning in class and other settings (see the case study below for more examples).

Linking back to the previous chapter, one example where curiosity and responsible learning emerge together is through unstructured play. Through games and self-led discoveries, adventurous learning begins. As Danks and Schofield (2005) point out, 'the natural world is a place for exploration, learning about risk, building confidence and escaping into imagination' (p. 10). We would add that these sorts of experiences could take place equally well in school grounds and urban green spaces. The key point is that through local outings, students can gain the tools with which to go on their own curiosity-driven adventures without being overly dependent on their teachers.

It is not just through unstructured activity that responsible learners develop, however. Bilton (2010) argues that while some subjects are better taught, others are better discovered independently. Either way, he notes that there are times when children need clear adult input in order to reach their potential. One way in which children can reach this potential in the outdoors is through responsible risk-taking (see also Chapter 8).

It is often assumed that 'traditional' outdoor educators are masters of working with risk through adventurous activities. While this may be true to some extent, in other ways nothing could be further from the truth. As experienced outdoor educators, the three of us have led many climbing and abseiling sessions. In every case, there are so many layers of safety equipment and procedures that little inherent adventure remains. As death cannot be a tolerable possibility, adventurous programmes (quite rightly) cannot devolve large amounts of genuine responsibility to children. Unless the leader makes an unlikely, catastrophic mistake, there is no occasion when the children are at significant risk. The degree to which participants *perceive* themselves as being at risk is quite another matter and not for discussion here. For the purposes of fostering responsible learners, and on the basis of the criteria above, the learning in the rock-climbing example above is not intrinsically-motivated, consequential, or student-led.

HOW CAN TEACHERS PLAN TO HELP THEIR STUDENTS BECOME RESPONSIBLE LEARNERS?

A contemporary view of outdoor learning means that school teachers need not encumber themselves with the barriers identified by Higgins, Nicol, and Ross (2006), when they researched teachers' perceptions of outdoor education (e.g. cost, time, ratios, safety, weather, transport, disruption to classes, and qualifications). Instead, when the vision of outdoor learning begins with developing responsible learners, not only do these barriers disappear, but the focus on the learners themselves addressing some of these obstacles provides new opportunities that exist much closer to home – all of which can be managed by school teachers. The crux in developing responsible learners in the outdoors is the compelling nature of direct experience, where bodily experiences can be directly related to cognitive thinking, and the learning that takes place outdoors can be linked to that taking place indoors. For this to happen we have to deliberately plan to make 'taking responsibility' a theme in our work. Teachers can do this by constructing situations that require decisions to be made by children where they realize the implications of their actions.

As we have seen, the environmental backdrop in which learning takes place affects children in different ways (Bilton, 2010). This is important because, while this chapter has focused mainly on how the environment can engender physical prompts to encouraging responsibility for self, Chapters 3 and 4 show how individuals can develop responsibility for the environment. Consequently, outdoor learning offers these different opportunities for developing responsibility where space and time are experienced very differently.

In the outdoors, where the stimuli are different from indoors, children can be physically active, cognitively engaged, experiencing emotions, and problem-solving in interdependent groups, all at the same time. There are also opportunities for children to increase their independence, develop their self-sufficiency, and promote their self-confidence. This development can be elicited through taking responsibility for their own learning in an environment where they assess their own risk, and the consequences of their actions are often direct and easily attributable to the actions that caused them. In the outdoors, where cause and effect are so obviously linked, learning becomes very personal.

CASE STUDY

Jane was fresh from teacher training college and had just begun her first teaching position at school. She was full of the ideas of Vygotsky, Piaget, Rogers, and others and was also a keen outdoors person. At university she was unable to find texts that linked these ideas with outdoor learning. This remained a puzzle to her because responsibility for learning had been a key theme of these theorists, and her own experiences in the outdoors reminded her of the breadth and depth of learning opportunities available to the committed learner – everything from being responsible for your own safety to learning in and from outdoor places.

Jane found out that her principal was keen to develop outdoor learning provision and she volunteered to help. The principal also asked Jane to work with an experienced teacher and write a short outdoor learning plan that linked theory and practice.

Jane's mentor suggested that they start with developing a template for a Personal Learning Plan (PLP).[2] Over the years, he had found PLPs to be particularly useful, as they are intended to nurture and monitor independent learning habits across all school subjects and are an ideal way to link outdoor learning with indoors. Central to PLPs is that students are involved in the planning and assessment of their own learning. Following this approach, Jane discussed the possibility of outdoor learning with her class and they were very enthusiastic.

Jane suggested to her class of 27 9-year-olds the curriculum topic of 'minibeasts' (e.g. invertebrates such as bugs, beetles, etc.). First, she wanted to establish *what they already knew* about the topic and conducted a brainstorm session, recording the information on a public display. From this activity, Jane then asked each child to think about and write down *something they would like to learn* about minibeasts. Remembering Vygotsky's ideas on cooperative learning, Jane aimed to develop teacher and learner responsibilities whilst nurturing a collaborative learning community.

One of the students pointed out to Jane that she had never seen minibeasts in the school grounds. Jane was aware of this and asked why this might be. The questions she used were intended to get the children thinking about habitat, ecosystems, life cycles, species identification, and

2 For more information on the thinking behind Personal Learning Plans see www.
   scotland.gov.uk/Publications/2004/09/19946/42934

food-webs, so that they could begin asking their own questions, such as 'Is it true that there is no life in the school grounds?' and 'If that is so, what changes in the grounds would encourage minibeasts to live there?'

In the absence of a suitable habitat, the solution to studying minibeasts in the school grounds was to create one. Jane now had enough information to begin work with the class in developing their individual tasks, such as developing their cognitive learning about the science topics they have already identified. Bearing in mind Piaget's guidance on 'age and stage' and Vygotsky's Zone of Proximal Development, Jane worked hard to make sure that the learning plans catered for differentiated learning. She also drew on an important aspect of cooperative learning: not all groups need to learn about the same things. A group can become 'experts' in one particular area and then share their learning with other groups. This approach gives all students, irrespective of their academic ability, opportunities to learn something collaboratively and to share their knowledge with others.

One very important task remained: how was the class going to construct the habitat for the minibeasts that they wanted to study? After some research, the class decided that the habitat they would like to create was a log pile. This would involve sourcing and transporting materials, and lead to other questions such as 'Who will do the work?', 'Will we need to do a risk assessment?', and 'Will it cost us money and, if so, where will it come from?'

Once the log pile was established, each individual began their own experiments based on the individual learning tasks they previously set for themselves in the classroom. Jane helped them develop topic webs so that the original questions led to other questions and the answers to these questions in turn led to even more questions. Over time, Jane developed a learning culture that moved indoors, then out, and back in again – thus allowing children to develop their learning in physical, intellectual, and emotional domains. Furthermore, she was able to broaden the theme of responsibility to include not just self, but others, and the environment that sustains us all.

Jane reviewed learning episodes with the children on the basis of agreed criteria and expectations, and highlighted the strong focus on a shared approach between her and the class. In this way, success and accountability can be demonstrated by students sharing their work with individual classmates, small groups, the entire class, or even the whole school.

Fully exploring what responsible learning is, and how responsible learners can be nurtured in the context of outdoor learning, is beyond the scope of this short chapter. As we have seen, taking responsibility for learning can be nurtured outdoors as well as indoors. This is good news for school teachers because, through their own training and teaching experience, they already possess many of the skills required to develop outdoor learning. However, something special about the outdoors provides learning opportunities that cannot easily be developed indoors.

The outdoors is a more reliably multi-dimensional learning space than the indoors, and provides situations that require children to consider different courses of action and then make decisions – the consequences of which will directly affect themselves and others. Engaging, meaningful education requires moving into territory where learning outcomes are not always pre-determined but brokered between learner and teacher in such a way that the responsibility for learning is shared by all parties.

GUIDELINES

- Some of the most respected thinkers in teaching and learning have identified responsibility as a key theme in student-centred learning.
- Using this knowledge, teachers can focus on responsibility as a unifying theme that allows them to integrate indoor learning with outdoor learning.
- For learning to be truly student-centred and multi-sensory, children need to have opportunities in the outdoors where they make their own decisions, experience the consequences, reflect on the outcomes, and then plan future courses of action.
- Because of the multi-dimensional nature of the outdoors, where outcomes can be uncertain, the influences on learning can be direct, obvious, immediate, and enduring.

Chapter 7

Building community partnerships

CHAPTER AIMS

- Understand curricular and non-curricular (societal) rationales for community-based learning.
- Recognize that the two principal features of community-based education (the provision of 'sites' and 'staff') offer valuable out-of-school learning opportunities.
- Be aware that four key approaches appropriate to working with individuals and agencies in the community are valuable in enhancing student learning.

WHAT IS LEARNING THROUGH COMMUNITY PARTNERSHIPS?

Learning through community partnerships is yet another approach to bringing learning outside the classroom to familiar, meaningful sites in children's neighbourhoods. Melaville, Berg, and Blank (2006) explain that the aim of such an approach is 'to more fully engage young people, by harnessing their natural interest in where and how they live and by using their own community as a source of learning and action' (p. 2). They go on to claim that 'the assets of a community – its history, culture, resources, and challenges – can help schools build citizens while infusing academic course work with meaning and relevance' (p. 31).

Two points distinguish community-based learning from other approaches. The first is obvious, in that 'Agencies and workplaces become potential sites for student learning' (Smith & Sobel, 2010, p. 23). Second, community members play a direct role in the educational process. This way, the wide range of inhabitants in the community become co-educators along with the teacher. In a traditional model of education, the classroom teacher is often seen as 'imparter of knowledge', whereas in a more integrated approach, as we saw in Chapters 5 and 6, the teacher's role shifts towards one of facilitator, with community members contributing (as appropriate) to children's learning.

As with all of the themes put forward in this book, we make the assumption that learning in and with the local community adds both curricular and pedagogical value to a child's schooling. As we shall see, the education of the student is only part of the overall rationale for community-based education.

WHY IS COMMUNITY-BASED EDUCATION IMPORTANT?

Melaville et al. (2006) note that 'students' own communities, whether rich or poor, provide a natural context for learning that matters to children' (p. 11). However, enhanced, more meaningful learning may not be the only reason for building partnerships between classes and community agencies. Although we are obviously focusing on young people's education, one can also make the argument that our communities and societies can benefit greatly from strong networks between students, parents, schools, and local businesses, government and charitable organizations.

Ife (2010) explains that there appears to be a common, cross-cultural story of communities being richer, more supportive, and more vibrant in decades past. Indeed, he notes that the

> Loss of community may have brought the benefits of industrialisation, mobility and wealth at a level undreamed of by the villagers of yesteryear, but in the modern mind these benefits were purchased at a loss of something valuable in terms of personal relationships, collective responsibilities and social cohesion.
>
> (p. 10)

Relationships and individuals' responsibilities to nurture those relationships are a crucial feature of healthy communities.

Smith (2002) goes on to explain that a community- and place-based approach to learning

> serves to strengthen children's connections to others and to the regions in which they live. It enhances achievement, but, more important, it helps overcome the alienation and isolation of individuals that have become hallmarks of modernity. By reconnecting children with, rather than separating them from, the world place-based education serves both individuals and communities, helping individuals to experience the value they hold for others and allowing communities to benefit from the commitment and contributions of their members (p. 594).

The strong overlap between place- and community-based education is abundantly clear: meaningful community-based education programmes need to be firmly situated within participants' local communities, as opposed to taking place in distant, de-contextualized, and 'more exotic' environments. Kazuo Maeda (2005) has written about children's outdoor learning programmes in Japan that work with older people to learn traditional skills in the local neighbourhood. He is clear that 'Community-based outdoor education should be implemented in the participants' place of residence, not in an "invaluable" eco-system in another place' (p. 42).

Blank and Berg's (2006) work in the United States cites some of their own research which indicates that when 'core academic curriculum is tied to the community, removing the artificial separation between the classroom and the real world, student outcomes are improved' (p. 8). As we can see from Ife, Blank and Berg, Smith, and Maeda, the benefits of learning in and with communities benefits the communities themselves as well as students.

THE SOCIAL CAPITAL ARGUMENT

It is not unusual for conventional outdoor adventure education courses (usually focused on personal and social development of some kind) to ignore the communities in which they take place (Beames & Atencio, 2008). Brookes (2002) has been a prominent critic of educational programmes that regard the landscapes 'as empty sites on which to establish social or psychological projects' (p. 405). Nonetheless, there appears to be an increasing number of teachers who note that outdoor learning can play an important role in the development of social relations that benefit both individuals and their broader communities (Maeda, 2005; McKenzie & Blenkinsop, 2006).

More recent work on outdoor learning has discussed the notion of social capital (see for example Beames & Atencio, 2008). American sociologist Robert

Putnam (2000) has helped to popularize the idea that social networks have value to both individuals and groups. The word 'capital' conjures up a number of different images – most of which relate to money! However, as Beames and Atencio (2008) point out, 'although an individual can possess physical capital (such as a car) or financial capital (such as money), only a group or community can possess social capital' (p. 100). The key point here is that because of their membership within certain groups, individuals are able to gain personal benefits. Informal neighbourhood relationships and formalized community groups may share information and resources with each other, thus enabling individuals to benefit (Putnam, 2000). In the absence of these social networks, individuals are less likely to share information about a job opportunity, find the name and number of a reliable plumber, or borrow some hedge clippers.

Much of Putnam's research has focused on highlighting the relationship between communities with strong social networks and child development, cleaner and safer streets, economic prosperity, and health and happiness (Putnam, 2000, pp. 296–333). He explains that there are two kinds of social capital: *bonding* and *bridging*. Bonding is something that is internally generated within a particular group or community. Bridging, on the other hand, is more outward-looking, and is hallmarked by relationships between people in different social groups. Putnam claims that by reaching out to build networks across social divisions, bridging has the capacity to help individuals get ahead in all aspects of their lives.

Like all 'hot topics', social capital is an area of social theory that has seen much attention, and is not without its critics. Still, we believe that for teachers the concepts are compelling, as they make an implicit demand on us: we need to create opportunities for our students to interact with people who are not like themselves, on meaningful neighbourhood projects.

We believe that educational programmes of all kinds are capable of building bridging social capital by being integrated into the issues, relationships, and stewardship of their communities. Indeed, running any kind of educational programme outside of the classroom 'while ignoring the various families, businesses, public services, voluntary groups, and social groups in the communities where these programmes are situated may mean that rich opportunities for bridging social networks are being lost' (Beames & Atencio, 2008, p. 104).

As we have seen, social capital theory offers one rationale for community-based learning that extends beyond the scope of discussions centring on what students learn and how they learn it. For Ife (2010), the idea of community is much larger than a curriculum; it is about 'collective, mutual rights and responsibilities, membership and belonging . . . which are generally seen as diminished within the context of modern (or postmodern) industrial (or post-industrial) societies but are positively valued' (p. 12). Ife places particular importance on the idea of membership, as this 'implies not just a certain status but also rights, privileges, responsibilities, and some level of common purpose' (p. 11).

In terms of recapping this section, community-based education (and sustainability education for that matter) is informed by two kinds of rationale. The first posits that community-based learning will enable deeper and more meaningful inter-disciplinary learning of the subject areas: in other words, it will help students meet curricular aims more effectively. The second general rationale is not driven by curricular imperatives, but is hallmarked by the aim of nurturing and building formal and informal social networks between individuals and agencies in the neighbourhood. The premise of this rationale is that these strong networks provide all community members with greater opportunities for individual gain.

When building an educational relationship with the local community it is important that the needs of the community should not be placed in competition with curricular demands; this is not about choosing community development over mathematics or literacy. We would argue that the most meaningful educational ventures involve addressing central elements of the curriculum while, for example, trying to start a small enterprise, interview an elderly person, or grow vegetables. While it may not be a school's primary purpose to contribute to or even revitalize a community, it could be seen as rather short-sighted or narrowly focused if this was not a by-product of learning in the authentic context of a community. Schools are inherently rich sites for community interaction, and can be further exploited for the benefit of all – with a school board and community members who are willing and able to offer the necessary support.

Blank and Berg (2006) pose the question, 'Who is responsible for creating the conditions for learning?' Their response is that

> schools, families, and communities must work together to get the results that we all want for our nation's children. By bringing together the assets and resources of communities and families at schools to help support students, while ensuring that the school sees the community as an important partner and resource, we can truly develop and nurture the whole child.
>
> (p. 11)

So, how can teachers take concrete steps towards learning in and with the community?

HOW CAN TEACHERS INCORPORATE LEARNING THROUGH COMMUNITY PARTNERSHIPS INTO THEIR PLANNING?

Blank and Berg (2006) propose that 'educating the whole child requires the whole community' (p. 25). As the saying goes, 'it takes a village to raise a child'. Doing this, however, requires making the boundary between school and community much more permeable and mutually sustaining. Smith and Sobel's (2010) four ways of 'doing' community-based education can be a very helpful way of understanding how students can learn through other people and places within their community.

The first, cultural aspects of community life, can involve learning about the human story of their place that has evolved over time. Smith and Sobel (2010) note that 'when students embrace rather than ignore their own ancestry and traditions, they will be more likely to commit themselves to the difficult but rewarding work of making communities good places to live' (p. 47).

Addressing environmental issues within the neighbourhood can involve conserving or looking after a particular site (e.g. green space or concrete space) or growing food and plants. There is also scope for civic involvement, as high-lighted below. This could also mean, for example, working to make changes within the community regarding people's consumption and disposal of material goods. Smith and Sobel (2010) write about home places having non-human assets and how once 'children and youth value those assets, they are more likely to be disposed to care for and protect them' (p. 47).

A third approach to community-based education focuses on learning about business and economic development. Although learning about global macro-economics has its place, Smith and Sobel (2010) argue that 'young people must also gain an understanding of what is required to make a living in the places where they live' (p. 51). Indeed, they report that some particularly enterprising schools in the United States have become 'genuine contributors to the economic well-being of the communities whose tax dollars support them' (p. 51). This has resonance with what, in Scotland, has been labelled 'enter-prising teaching and learning'.[1] While this refers to an overall creative and enterprising approach to education, it does incorporate entrepreneurship and work-based learning, as appropriate.

The fourth and final approach to community-based education is perhaps the most important, as it focuses on young people taking responsibility for the well-being of something bigger than themselves and the school. Healthy

---

1 See http://www.ltscotland.org.uk/learningteachingandassessment/learningacrossthe curriculum/themesacrosslearning/enterprise/about/enterprisingteaching.asp

societies require young people to take a proportionate share of the responsibilities that accompany the rights of adulthood. While popular conceptions of democracy may focus on the national and global, Smith and Sobel emphasize civic involvement that is 'aimed at inducting young people into the give and take of local decision-making' (p. 54). This way, 'students develop the knowledge, skills, and attributes of effective citizenship by identifying and acting on issues and concerns that affect their own community' (Melaville et al., 2006, p. 3). Smith (2002) calls this approach 'real-world' problem solving, as its curriculum 'is deeply grounded in particular places and highly democratic in its processes' (p. 589). Delivering the curriculum in ways that are 'couched' in citizenship can be managed throughout a young person's formal schooling.

We see especially strong links between learning outside the classroom and Smith and Sobel's (2010) four approaches to community-based education. In our own work, we refer to these approaches as culture, nature, enterprise, and citizenship. We suggest that another element can be more deliberately incorporated into citizenship: service. Although the term 'citizenship' may encapsulate all that is service, we believe that it is important to be clear that service is about responding to other people's specific needs. Without this element, citizenship can be limited in its conception and be seen as something that is hallmarked entirely by people identifying the issues that they want to address through democratic processes. This, in itself, is notable, but there is room for more!

There is arguably a certain power surrounding service. As Kurt Hahn, the driving force behind Outward Bound, once said to a colleague:

> There are three ways of trying to win the young. There is persuasion. There is compulsion. There is attraction. You can preach at them; that is a hook without a worm. You can say 'You must volunteer'; that is the devil. And you can tell them, 'You are needed.' That appeal hardly ever fails.
>
> (Stetson, n.d., p. 8)

Service learning as a subject area is particularly well-developed in the United States of America. Butin (2010) explains that it 'is seen as both a pedagogy and a philosophy that links classrooms with communities and textbooks with the 'real world' (p. xiv). It is clearly linked to community-based education, as it 'embraces the possibilities of conjoint civic renewal' (p. xiv). Butin is concerned about the 'classroom as graveyard – rows and rows of silent bodies' and urges teachers to embrace 'an active pedagogy committed to connecting theory and practice, schools and community, the cognitive and the ethical' (p. 3).

Perhaps the most important principle of service learning is that 'those doing the service should always be respectful of the circumstances, outlooks, and ways of those being served' (Butin, 2010, p. 5). Indeed, those being served should be the ones articulating what the service should be.

In 2002, Smith explained the educational power associated with what he termed 'real world problem-solving'. This involves 'engaging students in the identification of school or community issues that they would like to investigate and address' (p. 589): students identify a community problem, select one on which the class can focus, study its characteristics and come up with possible solutions, and then marshal efforts to solve the problem. The teacher's job is to facilitate this process by 'linking the problem to the required curriculum, finding resources, and acting as a general troubleshooter' (p. 590).

CHALLENGES OF COMMUNITY PARTNERSHIPS

There are two common challenges to building community partnerships for educational purposes: child protection and finding a willing agency partner.

Media attention to issues surrounding child protection has greatly escalated in the last decade (see, for example, Furedi & Bristow, 2008). Furedi and Bristow's research describes how our communities have been weakened by a culture that suspects volunteers, coaches, and other helpful parents as potential child abusers until they have undergone a criminal disclosure. They argue that involving other adults in the socialization and development of young people is not a new concept. Indeed, the 'evidence of history indicates that one of the ways that communities are forged has been through the joint commitment of adults to the socialisation of children' (p. xiii). In most communities, all of the adults 'are expected to introduce children into the norms of the community, protect them against hazards and if necessary reprimand anti-social behaviour' (p. xiii).

While we do not mean to trivialize the subject of child abuse, we would argue that the potential risks are manageable and that instances are very rare in educational settings. Certainly, in the UK, it is perfectly reasonable for adults in the community (who have not been officially vetted) to work with children on an occasional or supervised basis. Both adults and students should protect themselves by not being alone, one-to-one. Child protection is a real concern, of course, but the benefits for students working with others in the community (and for the community itself) are very significant.

The second main obstacle when developing a community-based education programme is in finding an organization or agency that is willing to work with your class. Part of your argument for this approach to learning is that as well as providing your students with an enriched educational experience in an authentic context, this will also benefit the agency. This 'exchange of services' might, for example, include low-cost labour to plant trees in exchange for a lesson on photosynthesis, and woodland management from the arborist.

Smith (2002) argues that 'organizations outside of the school, including businesses, must come to see themselves as partners in the education of children' (p. 594). It can certainly be challenging for school classes to find agencies that are willing to enter a partnership with them. The rewards of 're-situating learning within the context of communities' (p. 594), for students, agencies, and the community as a whole, are, we believe, too important to miss.

Melaville et al. (2006) advise schools to 'seek mutually beneficial relationships with community partners who have expertise to share and publicly recognize the assets they bring to student learning and civic development' (p. 28). There are now countless examples of schools that have formed partnerships with countryside rangers, bakeries, garden centres, police forces, medical clinics, hotels, charities, homeless shelters, and churches.

Effective community-based education programmes are able to provide participants with opportunities to work on projects involving face-to-face interactions with strangers. Accordingly, Ife (2002) stresses the importance of building relationships across social divides, as 'the more people who are active participants, the more ideals of community ownership and inclusive process will be realized' (p. 219). Programmes aiming to transform communities must foster opportunities for individuals to work and play with one another.

British outdoor education consultant, Juliet Robertson, suggests being quite deliberate about capitalizing on the knowledge, skills, and interests of parents and families of children attending school. For example, when a child enrols in the school, part of the paperwork can include a brief section or questionnaire about the knowledge, skills, and interests of parents and carers. This information can be fed into a database so that when a class project happens, the school can see which parents might be able to contribute their expertise. Tactically, this approach works better than a general call out for volunteers in a newsletter.

Another idea that Juliet Robertson advocates is setting aside a staff meeting, wherein every staff member explores their local area on foot. Even for seasoned, local teachers, this 'revisiting' of local shops, services, and green spaces with the added lens of 'how can this bring the curriculum alive and enrich the local area', can be highly effective; the ways of building bridges between schools and their communities are innumerable.

CASE STUDY

Five years ago, teachers, parents, and administrators of Laurentian High School came to the conclusion that they were not doing enough to give their students every opportunity to learn and grow. Despite the fact that they were not doing anything poorly, it seemed illogical to the School Life Committee to think that a) teachers could be expected to possess the full depth and breadth of knowledge and skills that would cater to the myriad interests of the students, and b) the learning environments within the confines of the school could yield rich and varied opportunities to learn in 'real world' situations.

The Committee decided to consider Smith and Sobel's four approaches of 'culture, nature, enterprise, and citizenship'. After exploring the ways in which these approaches lent themselves to the needs of the local people and place, the decision was made to work with a nearby senior citizens' home. Their thinking was that they would start with one project that offered the flexibility of being able to draw on all four approaches, if necessary.

A two-pronged plan was developed. One grade 8 class was going to re-vamp the two main flower beds, and sand, prime, and paint the front door and the planter boxes on the windows. A grade 10 English class was going to interview the residents about how the community had evolved over the last 75 years.

The grade 8 class paid a visit to the site and took note of what tools they would need to borrow and what material they would need to buy. The seniors' home had a small budget for annual maintenance and this year the labour was free! The students were amazed at how many residents joined them for aspects of the work.

The teacher of the grade 10 class had been inspired by the Foxfire programme that began in America's Southern Appalachian region in 1966.[2] He suggested to his class that they work in pairs and put together a collection of stories that were based on interviews with the community elders who lived in the seniors' home. An anthology was written, edited, and printed as part of the students' English class, and served to further cement their cultural heritage by leaving a written legacy of the people who had shaped the community.

Curricular outcomes relating to science and ecology, math and technology, and language arts were obvious to the teachers, who assisted students with putting together their learning portfolios.

2 Learn more about the Foxfire program at http://www.foxfire.org/

The wide-ranging body of literature linking both community development and community-based education indicates two over-arching themes. First, communities need the young people who live and attend school in the local area to be actively engaged in ensuring that their 'place' puts a high value on nurturing relationships of trust and reciprocity between all members — both within and between subgroups — irrespective of background. Second, schooling that relies solely on classroom teachers as the only adults legitimately able to facilitate a young person's learning are limiting the capacity each student has to realize their full potential.

Communities are full of individuals and organizations able to act as partners and co-educators, as their children go about acquiring useful and relevant knowledge, skills, and attitudes. Healthy communities and community-engaged schooling are mutually supportive.

GUIDELINES

- When schools engage with the community, places outside of the classroom, such as agencies, businesses, and green-spaces, become sites of learning.
- A diverse range of members within the community — along with their varied skills and knowledge — can become regarded as educators.
- Ideally, a community's social networks will strengthen at the same time that students are learning in more authentic and meaningful contexts.

Chapter 8

Administration and risk management

CHAPTER AIMS

- Understand the basic principles associated with leading others outdoors.
- Be aware of the five elements of a basic risk management plan and be able to construct plans for outdoor learning.
- Recognize and be able to devise ways in which students can be involved in managing the hazards they might encounter.

WHAT IS RISK MANAGEMENT?

In simple terms, risk management involves assessing and – where appropriate – taking action to reduce the risks that arise from activities. It may sometimes mean reducing the likelihood and severity of adverse outcomes, or even removing hazards entirely. However, consider what any educational programme would look like (whether indoors or out) if all of the risk were to be removed! Our students might be subjected to learning in individual rooms with blank walls and no other objects. The chance of students hurting themselves is greatly reduced, but so too is the opportunity to learn. If we take an empty room as the starting point and then move out along the spectrum of what we believe is important to expose our students to, where will we end up? Paradoxically, as we will see, there are likely to be even greater risks associated with children being exposed to such sterile and un-stimulating environments.

As you're reading this book, we assume that you will end up outside the classroom for some of the time, as the classroom is ultimately limited in its capacity to foster real-world interaction with people and place. An 'as safe as possible' ethos inevitably means that opportunities to learn in authentic contexts in an experiential manner will be severely limited. If teachers believe in the power of learning outside the classroom, they need to understand and apply basic risk management practices, and feel supported by the growing body of experts in this field.

A helpful starting point is to distinguish between a *hazard* and a *risk*. A hazard is anything with the potential to cause harm. A risk refers to the likelihood and severity of being harmed by a hazard. Risk assessment, therefore, is the process of considering these possibilities (Barton, 2007, p. 12).

Research has shown that it is common for teachers to be highly concerned about issues of negligence and liability when accompanying their students outside the school grounds (see for example, Ross et al., 2007). A significant part of risk management involves conducting a 'formal assessment of the foreseeable risks that might be met on an excursion . . . [with] the aims of preventing the risks or reducing them' (Scottish Executive, 2004, p. 13). This can be tricky ground for teachers as, of course, it is impossible to foresee every outcome that might harm a child in their care (more on this in Chapter 9).

In most jurisdictions, whether indoors or outdoors, teachers have a duty to provide a *standard of care* that is commensurate with 'what other reasonable and prudent professionals would do in similar situations' (Martin, Cashel, Wagstaff, & Breunig, 2006, p. 255). As Gill (2010) notes, 'The notion of reasonableness is central to the key legislation' (p. 12). A reasonable and prudent teacher would complete a risk assessment for any outdoor learning sessions that took place in the local neighbourhood or for any sessions that took place in the school grounds that were different from normal school ground activities (e.g. running around, playing with soccer balls and skipping ropes). A reasonable and prudent teacher might also deem it necessary to alter the plan in the face of circumstances that have changed. For example, the walking route to the Town Hall may have to be changed if there is some construction work blocking the way.

Another legal term feared by many schools and teachers is *negligence*. Negligence can be simply defined as 'a wrong committed by one person against another' (Gregg, 2005, p. 193). In technical terms, 'wrongs' have four elements:

1   Duty: the legal responsibility to act as a reasonable professional.
2   Breach of that duty: failing to meet the standard of care.

3   Injury: harm must have been caused.

4   Causation: there must be a causal relation between the breach of duty and the injury.

American attorney Reb Gregg is an expert on legal issues surrounding outdoor activities and explains that the claim of negligence can only succeed in the courts if all of the above four elements are present (2005, p. 193).

The principal aim of this chapter is not, of course, to ensure that teachers know how to avoid being convicted of negligence. We want to ensure that teachers take a balanced, thoughtful, and enabling approach to what they must do as reasonable and prudent professionals who are taking their students outdoors in order to enhance their learning experiences.

WHY IS BEING APPROPRIATELY EXPOSED TO RISK IMPORTANT?

Tim Gill (2010) has written extensively on the subject of young people, risk, and the outdoors. He warns that:

> A mindset that is solely focused on safety does children and young people no favours. Far from keeping them safe from harm, it can deny them the very experiences that help them to learn how to handle the challenges that life may throw at them. There is an emerging consensus that our society has become too focused on reducing or eliminating risk in childhood.
>
> (Gill, 2010, p. 1)

Gill goes on to quote the Chair of the UK's Health and Safety Executive, who stated that 'If the next generation enter the workplace having been protected from all risk they will not be so much be risk averse as completely risk naive' (p. 1). There appears to be risk in not exposing our students to risks!

Scottish outdoor risk management expert Bob Barton (2007) states that there is a central paradox to notions of risk within contemporary society: 'We are increasingly insulated from physical harm, yet are becoming more and more risk averse' (p. 2). Concerns have been raised by sociologist Frank Furedi (2002), who argues that fear has become an 'ever-expanding' part of Western life and that a 'consequence of this atmosphere of fear is that many parents are no longer prepared to trust other adults to look after their children' (p. xi).

79

This culture of fear raises fascinating questions for school teachers. For example:

- Should we try to eliminate risk?
- Are some risks tolerable?
- Do we have a duty to expose children to risks?

There is always some chance that a student could trip and fall down the stairs or a small airplane could crash into the classroom. If we tried to minimize all risk and wrapped our students in cotton wool and confined them to the classroom for their entire formal schooling, would we then be guilty of denying them important learning opportunities that exist beyond the four walls of the classroom? We suspect that even the most conservative, risk averse teacher would concede that their students would be exposed to more opportunities to learn across the curriculum if they spent some of their formal schooling outside the classroom.

If we follow this logic, we would perhaps concede that some risks are tolerable. An example of this kind of risk might be something that has a low level of severity (e.g. being scratched by a branch on a tree in the school ground) or has a low likelihood of happening (e.g. lightning striking a student). Indeed, Scotland's *Curriculum for excellence through outdoor learning* states that 'Children and young people should not be denied an experience simply because some significant but unlikely hazard could not be completely eliminated' (Learning and Teaching Scotland, 2010, p. 24).

Gill (2007) summarizes four main arguments for risk being something that is desirable, rather than something to be avoided. First, encounters with risks help children to learn how to manage risks that they will face through their lifetime (e.g. traffic, canals). Second, children have an appetite for risk that needs to be fed. If it is not fed, this may lead to children seeking out opportunities for much greater risk-taking. Third, children gain health and developmental benefits from being more physically active (as opposed to playing video games indoors). Finally, the fourth argument is that children develop resilience through facing up to adverse circumstances. The trouble with these four reasons for deliberately exposing children to risks as part of an educational programme is that they are very difficult to measure. Conversely, measuring the number of students who hurt themselves in the classroom, school grounds, or beyond the school grounds is relatively easy. Still, there appears to be increasing attention given to the value of young people being exposed to hazards – particularly those which will be faced over a lifetime, such as road traffic or heavy rain.

If schools have a role to play in the development of the whole person, it is arguable that teachers have a duty to expose their students to tolerable risks –

especially if this gives students the chance to learn how to assess and manage risk. So, if we are going to educate in the school grounds and local neighbourhood as a means of enriching learning, it follows that both teachers and students should develop the skills with which to manage risks. The duty to expose students to appropriate degrees of risk then becomes a moral requirement, and learning outside the classroom becomes an educational imperative.

We will now examine five key tools that can form part of teachers' risk management plan: risk assessments, emergency action plans, consent forms, off-site checklists, and incident reporting. Naturally, these elements will vary between school districts, regions, and countries.

RISK ASSESSMENTS

Risk assessments are a legal requirement in many circumstances. Even when not required by law, they are often stipulated by local authorities and other bodies.

The good news is that risk assessments for learning in the school grounds and local neighbourhood can be much more straightforward than those for rock-climbing or white-water kayaking! Our risk assessments do not need to be complex, nor require technical formulae. Indeed, Gill (2010) notes that quantitative risk assessments with scoring and arithmetic 'can be confusing and difficult to apply consistently' and may 'struggle to cope with the subtleties and dilemmas thrown up by real-life situations' (p. 16).

In outdoor learning contexts, three general kinds of risk assessment tend to be used: *generic*, *specific*, and *dynamic* (adapted from Barton, 2007). *Generic risk assessments* cover hazards that one can expect to encounter on most ventures outside of the classroom. In local settings, these typically involve the 'big three': exposure (to wind, precipitation, sun, and cold); vehicular traffic (when crossing or walking beside roads); and terrain (e.g. conditions under-foot, steep slopes, water features). Of course, depending on the context and region, other hazards may be environmental or external (e.g. being bitten by a snake if in the countryside, or students being separated from the group in a big city).

Event specific risk assessments often exist as 'add-ons' to *generic risk assessments*. For example, let's say that walking to any site within a one-mile radius of the school was part of the generic risk assessment. Now, if the class was involved in an environmental project that necessitated using saws and secateurs to clear bushes, it is obvious that this is beyond what could normally be expected to happen on a visit to the park. However, a specific risk assessment can be written that outlines how the hazards presented by using these tools can be adequately controlled. A specific risk assessment, then, may be employed for a certain activity, location, or group – or perhaps a combination of the three.

Where they are required, generic and specific assessments should be completed well in advance and approved by the head of school or designated health and safety advisor. It is important to note that generic risk assessments can be written once and amended as appropriate: a new generic assessment does not have to be written before each outing. The same can be said of specific risk assessments. If, upon reflection, the secateurs and saws assessment was adequate for the first session, it will presumably be suitable for the following one.

The third kind of risk assessment is dynamic. *Dynamic risk assessments* are ongoing and are usually not written down. In most cases it is a question of having all of your senses constantly alert in order to gather as much information as possible about the surrounding environment. Teachers working outdoors need to be considering changes in weather; students' physical, mental, emotional condition; terrain 'under foot'; and crossing points for road, rail or water. Dynamic risk assessment is really about the judgement derived from an inner dialogue or from regular check-ins with a class assistant, other adults, and the children within the group – the result of which may be a change of plan or abandoning the outing altogether. An example of this could be (as mentioned earlier in the chapter) altering the walking route if there was construction on the sidewalk, or not using the saws to cut bushes if one of the volunteers, needed to ensure a suitably high adult to student ratio, didn't show up.

Sadly, an element of most generic and dynamic risk assessments that should be carefully considered is the threat, albeit unlikely, of unwanted visitors. Intimidating teenagers showing up on the school grounds and over-friendly adults asking children for their names and addresses are valid concerns. These hazards should be considered in relation to the personal circumstances of the children in each class, as well as the people who are likely to be encountered during class outings.

In their simplest form, generic risk assessments and specific risk assessments generally include two columns: hazard and control measure. An excerpt from a generic risk assessment for walking to sites within the close proximity of a semi-urban primary school in Canada could be as in Table 8.1.

Obviously, there is room to add in other hazards. One example could be ice patches, which could come under the hazard heading of 'terrain'. However, since (in the example in Table 8.1) students may be exposed to patches of ice in their school grounds and in aspects of their life outside of school, one could argue that this was not necessary. Further consideration might highlight that, for a group of individuals with behaviour issues, horse-play on the ice might be seen as a hazard that is quite likely and that could have very serious consequences.

Table 8.1 Generic risk assessment for walking to sites within the close proximity of a semi-urban primary school in Canada

Hazard	Control measure
Road traffic	• Students all wear high visibility vests. • Roads are only crossed at 'green man' road crossings. • Students walk two-by-two on the sidewalk and will be mindful of allowing other pedestrians to pass.
Exposure to elements	• Students wear clothing and footwear appropriate to the conditions. Extra layers should be brought with them in case conditions change. Staff also carry spare items of clothing.

Common sense is needed to decide whether or not particular risks or hazards need to be considered in a risk assessment. The risk assessment process can, in the hands of the anxious, be almost infinitely extended by the addition of unlikely or trivial risks – a problem that the UK's Health and Safety Executive has recognized in its guidance on sensible risk management.[1] Used thoughtfully, risk assessments can help to ensure that classes can be outdoors in poor weather or unusual conditions; even if managing the circumstances appears straightforward, the absence of such an assessment may mean having to staying indoors unnecessarily.

The main point we are making is that risk assessments should not be downloaded from the Internet and used uncritically; they should be specifically designed to suit the specific people, places, and activities involved. By all means, ask for help from fellow teachers and experts in the school district. Indeed, we suggest that risk assessments should be created through shared discussions from all staff involved in the activity. Risk assessments are about developing sensible routines and procedures, and need to be living documents – not simply bits of paper that are written down to 'get the job done' and then left in a filing cabinet at school.

EMERGENCY ACTION PLAN

An 'emergency action plan' is a brief, readily accessible flow-chart that can guide action in a time of adrenaline-filled stress. We recommend fitting this and the risk assessment on to one sheet of paper, putting it into a clear waterproof case, and bringing it with you on each outing. By using a case and not laminating

1 See the HSE website: www.hse.gov.uk/risk/principlespoints.htm

the paper, teachers are able to amend these documents as appropriate – thus demonstrating their constant re-evaluation of their risk management practices. As well as being useful effective teaching tools, waterproof paper and grease pencils in your off-site kit also ensure that you are able to make notes in the event of a crisis in wet weather.

Broadly speaking, crises can be categorized as *life-threatening* and *non-life-threatening*. So, an incident involving a boy who has fallen from a rocky step and is unconscious would be handled differently if he had only hurt his ankle. Consider how the following questions might be addressed in the two scenarios:

- How can I ensure that uninjured members of the group are not harmed?
- Who will administer first aid?
- Who will I call first?
- Who will manage the group?

It makes good sense to establish roles among the adults in the group before starting out. So, for example, if there were three adults for the class of 27:

- one assistant could ensure any other students descending the rocky step get down safely;
- one may have to administer basic life support (or treat the injured ankle);
- and you as teacher could call emergency services first and the head of school second (for the unconscious child) (or call the head of school in order to discuss appropriate options for the child with the suspected ankle sprain).

Whether it is the head of school who is contacted or not, what is crucial is that there is a designated 'home base' contact. This person is usually an administrator who will be at school (or contactable on a dedicated, switched-on phone after school hours) while your class is out. Their responsibility is to provide assistance as necessary. They will have a written plan of where you have gone and the details of who has gone with you. In some cases they may, if appropriate, notify parents. Additionally, they may be able to garner the assistance of community partners in your area.

One further consideration has become a modern issue in crisis management: cell phones. In the event of a more serious accident, it may be advisable to collect students' personal phones so that no inaccurate and potentially damaging information is fed to other parents and community members. For example, the ankle sprain in the example above can rapidly become a traumatic, life-threatening injury in an emotionally charged phone call from an observing student to a parent, who in turn phones another parent, and so on.

Best practice is for the communication with parents and media to be undertaken by the designated, trained home-base contact. Particularly serious incidents require attention by the designated senior member. If for some reason it cannot be helped that you are the one to share information, this information should be restricted exclusively to facts. Opinion and speculation have no place in the immediate aftermath of an incident. Certainly, no students' names should be shared with anyone from the media. School districts will have guidance for dealing with the media, and can suitably advise on protocol.

Irrespective of whether the incident was minor or major, ensure that you write down an account of all events and times, as soon as possible. This can be a useful document for any future enquiry or risk management review. Most school districts will have incident forms that include accidents and near misses. In many countries, organizations are required to report any serious injuries to their equivalent of their government agency responsible for health and safety.

CONSENT FORMS

Most schools are very familiar with consent forms (also known as 'permission slips') for parents and carers. These written forms are required for any off-campus outing and for non-routine activities that take place within the school grounds. A style of consent form that is becoming more common is a 'blanket' consent form that covers a variety of low risk, curricular activities that are taking place in the school grounds or local neighbourhood for the duration of the academic year.

Blanket consent forms can greatly reduce the amount of bureaucracy associated with taking children outside of the classroom. Since these forms remove the need for parental consent for each outing, more spontaneous and serendipitous teaching and learning can occur.

Both blanket and event-specific consent forms need to cover the following:

- the nature of the activity;
- the benefits of the activity (i.e. educational rationale);
- times, dates, locations;
- what to bring (any food, drink, clothing);
- an acknowledgement that all outings involve students being exposed to certain risks that are different from those inside the classroom;

- assurance that a risk assessment has been conducted and that an emergency action plan is in place;
- accompanying staff and experience/competence;
- room for parents to highlight any medical concerns and emergency contact numbers;
- room for parents to sign and date the form.

It may be that the blanket consent form can cover the majority of local off-site activity for an entire academic year. For example, the same consent form may cover walking to a local park, taking the public bus to the museum, or gardening within the school grounds. Unusual, one-off events (e.g. a sponsored mountain walk to raise money for charity) and overnight excursions of all kinds (e.g. going to Paris or going on an expedition) will demand much more comprehensive risk assessments and specific consent forms.

OFF-SITE CHECKLISTS

The off-site checklist can be a laminated form that is kept next to the 'off-site backpack' (more on this in Chapter 9). This checklist is not necessarily a list of what must be done before leaving the classroom or what must be brought along, but rather, what should be considered. These considerations generally include:

1 The off-site kit: first aid kit, medication, the risk assessment document, consent forms, emergency action plan,[2] group shelter.
2 A 'tucker bag': possibly with food, drink, cups, plates, and effective hand cleaning materials.
3 Checking the weather forecast.
4 Considering boundaries and instructions for the journey to the site, as well for the site itself.
5 Notifying the school office where the class is going, which adults are going, when you plan to return, and your cell phone number.
6 Ensuring that students go to the toilet before leaving the school.
7 Ensuring that children know who their assigned adult and 'buddies' are for the outing.

2 This assumes that leaders will bring their own cell phones.

INCIDENT REPORTING AND MONITORING

Barton (2007) prefers the term 'incidents' to refer to adverse occurrences. This broader term is about much more than accidents and can refer to accidents, illnesses, near misses, and behavioural incidents. All of these 'events' can be monitored as a means of building a fuller picture of the risks faced by the students and teachers who are learning outdoors. It is therefore considered good practice to keep written records of all incidents, as described above. This information should include people, locations, events, times, dates, and notable circumstances that featured. Incident reporting can be the fifth section of your risk assessment binder.

It is vital to create a culture of cooperation and learning around any incidents (whether indoors or out). A teacher who is worried about being reprimanded because one of her student's arms was bruised by rock fall, may not want to document the incident. The concern then becomes that other teachers won't learn from these events, and may then make the same decision to take the class near the bottom of the local cliff.

The rationale for such record-keeping is to identify trends in incidents, which may then lead to an improvement of risk management systems. These records can be particularly illuminating when compared with others providing similar experiences for their students. Importantly, records can be used as a means of demonstrating the risks associated with a specific activity very rarely result in harmful incidents. Another way to think of this is that incident monitoring is simply an extension of the learning and teaching process, and is something that teachers are already accustomed to doing as part of their daily routine.

'BUT WHAT HAPPENS IF SOMETHING DOES GO WRONG?'

A question that we are often asked in classes and in professional development courses is, 'If there is an accident, am I going to get into trouble?' Unsurprisingly, our answer to this question is, 'It depends'. It depends on whether or not you, as the teacher with the duty of care, have done what other reasonable and prudent colleagues would have done.

If a child was hit by an out-of-control car while you were walking to the museum, there would undoubtedly be an inquiry. The inquiry would hopefully show that you had done a thorough risk assessment, which included a section highlighting that students are instructed to walk along the sidewalk in pairs and to not go on to the street, except when crossing at a designated place in the agreed way. The evidence would also hopefully show that you had signed blanket consent forms for each child. In such circumstances, it would have been impossible for you to predict that a driver would lose control of their car and drive on to the sidewalk. Everything you did was what a reasonable and prudent person would do.

Speaking in 2007, Jonathan Rees of the UK's Health and Safety Executive stated that:

> It is worth pointing out that many of the concerns we read about health and safety are based on myths. For instance: HSE does not expect risk assessments for everyday low risk activities like playing conkers[3] and contrary to popular belief teachers are not personally sued for damages – we cannot find a single example of an individual teacher being sued in the past 5 years.
>
> (Health and Safety Executive, 2007, para 4)

Once the risks have been analyzed and unnecessary risks eliminated, Gregg (n.d.) states that the 'risks necessary to the achievement of clearly stated goals should be well managed' (para 3). This notion of certain risks being an integral part of a larger educational aim is vital, and resonates with an approach that is being promoted in Scotland (Learning and Teaching Scotland, 2010). They take a broader view of hazards and risks and see them in the greater context of educational benefit. This approach has been labelled a risk/benefit analysis that 'consciously balances the benefits of an experience against the intrinsic risks' (p. 24). They go on to state that those 'taking children and young people outdoors . . . should adopt an enabling attitude towards outdoor learning that identifies exciting, creative opportunities for learning' (p. 24).

The Learning and Teaching Scotland risk/benefit analysis poses three principal questions to teachers:

- What is the added value of this lesson taking place outside the classroom? (*educational benefits*)
- What risks have been identified as being significantly greater than those experienced in normal school life? How are they being managed? (*prominent risks*)
- How are the benefits in proper balance with any potential for harm? (*justification*)

---

3 Conkers is a British game that children have played for centuries, using the seeds of horse-chestnut trees. Players have a conker (the chestnut seed) threaded onto a piece of string and take turns striking each other's conker until one breaks.

Gill (2010) also advocates a more balanced approach which accepts a degree of risk that is properly managed (p. 2). He encourages teachers to view such risks as not only inevitable, but also as desirable. Furedi (2009) warns us against 'worst-case' thinking, where planning for the worst possible outcomes, rather than most probable outcomes, dominates our time and energy. He argues that:

> Worst-case thinking encourages society to adopt fear as of one of the dominant principles around which the public, its government, and institutions should organise their life. It institutionalises insecurity and fosters a mood of confusion and powerlessness.
>
> (p. 215)

It is important to be realistic, however, and recognize that 'outcomes, good or bad, cannot be completely determined in advance' (Gill, 2010, p. 7). Despite teachers' efforts to carefully prepare and act reasonably, accidents do happen on school outings, just as they do in everyday life. It follows that it is impossible for school teachers to offer guarantees of safety, whether indoors or outdoors. As Gregg (n.d.) notes, 'even good programmes will have accidents' (para 3). Should an accident occur, the 'focus should be on learning how and why it happened, and the prevention of a repeat occurrence' (para 3). Crucially, we need to remember that genuine accidents do happen: 'from time to time, terrible things happen and no-one is to blame' (Gill, 2010, p. 7). This is, of course, true in schools as well as in the outdoors.

The starting point for educational planning needs to centre directly on what students need to learn and the best ways for this to be learned. From there, risk/benefit analyses will be done to consider if the foreseen hazards are manageable.

GETTING STUDENTS INVOLVED

One point that is especially important to make is the importance of students taking some responsibility for managing the risk for their own outings. This is an important point because in sharing this responsibility, the children are actively engaged in looking after themselves, even though the teacher may at times have to make executive decisions. There is obvious overlap with Chapter 6 on student responsibility, but it is worth making the point again, as this approach has proven to be particularly powerful in our own partnership work with Scottish schools.

As we have indicated, it is the teacher's responsibility to ensure that bureaucratic necessities of consent forms, emergency action plans, and risk assessments are covered. Certainly, in a more 'old school' approach, this would have been more than adequate. However, if teachers really aspire to 'walk the talk' of empowering students, it is imperative that they facilitate the process that allows students to manage the risk for their own excursions. As they grow up, young people need to learn how to manage the risks inherent in their own journeys and adventures – experiences that sooner or later take place outside the watchful eye of their school teachers and parents.

Apart from the five elements of risk management that teachers need to address, it is crucial that students are assessing and managing hazards and taking responsibility for planning their outings. In our work, we have used two tools to great effect; both are completed by students, with the teacher's help.[4]

The first tool is the 'journey plan'. This is an outline highlighting who is involved, where the outing is going, when the group will be back, what is the dedicated cell phone number, and so on. It also has a checklist including (at the very least): a first aid kit (with any specific medicine), a copy of the journey plan taken to the office, extra warm layers, consent forms for all students, and a toilet strategy.

The second tool is a simple hazard assessment. At first we only look at those hazards that can seriously harm us and how they can be managed. For some age groups, introducing the concepts of the likelihood and severity of being harmed by that hazard may be too complex to begin with. These two elements of planning for outings can provide students with very concrete ways of taking responsibility for their own safety and learning (see Chapter 7).

CASE STUDY

Scott and Mary Kay are both Grade 3 teachers who decided to take their students' learning outdoors. One of the first things they needed to do was to put together a comprehensive risk management plan. The aim of the plan was not to remove the possibility of encountering hazards, but to reduce the likelihood of encountering any undesirable hazards and to put in place considered procedures for addressing those hazards that were perhaps greater in severity, though less likely to occur.

With the backing of their school principal, Scott and Mary Kay set about putting together a risk management plan. This 'living' document

---

4 The journey plan and the hazard assessment can be downloaded from www. outdoorjourneys.org.uk or made to measure in a way that suits you and your students.

would be kept at the school office, in the classroom, and in the off-site rucksack, and was always available for students, parents, and school inspectors to view. The document included five main elements: a generic risk assessment for outdoor learning in the school yard and local neighbourhood, an off-site checklist for the teacher in charge, an emergency action plan, a blanket consent form, and incident reporting.

Scott and Mary Kay took advice from the local health and safety officer, a principal who had overseen the process at a nearby school, and some helpful souls on an Internet forum for teachers who regularly worked outside the classroom. They took a few weeks to put together a binder with the five sections. The whole document was only eight pages long, in total.

Ultimately, risk management should focus on sensibly enabling, rather than nonsensically constraining. Paraphrasing legendary American pioneer of outdoor leadership, Paul Petzold, Martin et al. (2006) note that no set of rules in a risk management document 'can address every potential problem that a leader might encounter' (p. 261). They go on to state that:

> While rules and guidelines are useful, they should represent only one part of a more comprehensive approach to safety and risk management. Those who rely solely on rules or guidelines as a basis for decision making will eventually find themselves in a situation for which they are ill-prepared and for which the guidelines come up short.
>
> (Martin et al., 2006, p. 261)

Teachers can learn and use basic tools, like risk assessments, consent forms, and emergency action plans – all of which will enable them to more safely and confidently take their curriculum outdoors. Hopefully, reading this chapter has demystified the (at times) vague and thorny topic of risks and their relationship to a young person's education. We are also mindful that addressing risk management for learning outside the classroom can be daunting for some teachers. Chapter 10 provides an overview of some useful initial steps that can be taken to help teachers take more learning outdoors.

GUIDELINES

- Ensure that your risk management strategy comprises a blanket consent form, a generic risk assessment, an emergency action plan, an outings checklist, and a way of monitoring any incidents.
- Create opportunities for students to develop their own hazard assessments and journey plans.

Chapter 9

Supervising people outdoors

CHAPTER AIMS

- Understand the environmental, human, and external factors that may influence students when teaching outdoors.
- Recognize the difference between a stationary site and moving site and strategies for managing each.
- Be able to employ basic strategies for teaching concepts and sharing information with groups when environmental, human, and external factors may be competing for students' attention.

In the majority of classroom teaching scenarios, most aspects of the setting can be controlled by the teacher. To a reasonable degree, the physical objects (such as chairs and tables), the environmental conditions (weather), and the structure of social interactions, can be manipulated by the teacher and the school. Once we move the classroom outdoors, however, many of these fundamental elements are beyond the direct control of the teacher and pose rather different challenges.

Teachers need to employ measures that mitigate the influence of events over which they have little or no control. It may be stating the obvious, but responding to the environmental factors (e.g. wind, rain, sun), human factors (e.g. physiological changes in body temperature and hydration, additional support needs, group dynamics), and external factors (e.g. people not directly related to the learning session, road traffic), is a key skill that teachers need to develop. Students who are distracted by a cold wind or a busy road will almost certainly be less capable of fully engaging with any lesson than they might otherwise be.

This chapter is much less about 'theory into practice' and much more about the nuts and bolts of managing groups of people when outside the classroom. As you will see, where the previous chapter on administration and risk management was predominantly about what measures need to be in place before a group leaves the classroom, this chapter focuses entirely on managing groups once they have left the classroom. Generally speaking, this means travelling to and from a site and being at the site. Although careful planning will help to make learning outside the classroom sessions run smoothly, the added, constantly changing circumstances of being outdoors inevitably demand a reasonable degree of 'thinking on one's feet'.

In keeping with the ongoing, dynamic risk assessments explained in the previous chapter, teachers need to constantly have an eye on the weather, students' primary needs and behaviour, terrain 'under foot', and other outside influences – whether expected or unexpected.

HOW CAN TEACHERS INCORPORATE OUTDOOR GROUP SUPERVISION STRATEGIES INTO THEIR PLANNING?

As stated in the chapter on learning outcomes, the three broad categories that need to be managed by teachers working outdoors are environmental, external, and human factors. Notice how they connect with the risk assessments outlined in Chapter 8? These three categories and their respective themes underpin the basis of an overall strategy for leading groups outside – whether travelling together or delivering a teaching session. The environmental, external, and human categories are approached from a risk management viewpoint, but also from the perspective of how best to optimize learning, given the prevailing conditions.

Environmental factors: sun, wind, rain, temperature

Interestingly, it is the environmental factors that are often the most straightforward to deal with. We can always have a granola bar if hungry, take a swig of water if thirsty, and put on a woolly hat and do some exercise if cold.

Sun

Hot and/or tropical climates may demand brimmed hats, sunscreen, and perhaps even long, lightweight clothing. In some cases, it may be necessary to restrict time spent outside during the hottest part of the day. Hyperthermia can be debilitating, but is very avoidable if certain measures are taken (e.g. sun protection and adequate hydration). One way to ensure that everyone is drinking is to get the group together and make 'a toast' to all of their hard work and team skills: everyone holds up their bottles and has a good drink.

Teaching tips

- When explaining something, ensure that the sun is in your eyes and not the eyes of your students.
- If using sunglasses, be sure to use ones that allow others to see your eyes (rose or orange coloured). Having eye contact is very important.

Wind and rain

In temperate climes, wind-chill can quickly cool youngsters. Even if the ambient temperature is above zero degrees Celsius, the wind-chill may effectively lower this to below freezing. Being wet is another factor that can quickly cool the human body. Being wet in the wind is cause for even greater concern. All attempts should be made to both get out of the wind, and to limit how wet the students become.

Keep in mind that just because the wind blows, the temperature drops, or it starts to rain, this does not mean the session should be abandoned (unless of course there are obvious safety implications). Consider these changing conditions as ongoing management issues, in the same way that you constantly strive to manage good practice in the classroom.

The importance of adequate waterproof clothing and boots for keeping students dry cannot be over-stated. Indeed, in the UK, not having this basic gear is one of the most common reasons that teachers decide against taking their class outdoors. Gore-tex™ and other specialist materials are not needed for learning outside the classroom in the local neighbourhood. Quite often, just having long cagoule-type jackets (that come down to the knees) and some rubber boots allow a teacher to run sessions outdoors in light rain, windy conditions, or when the ground is wet. Jackets like these are also good for keeping students warmer in cold conditions.

Teaching tips

- If the rain appears to come in waves, take breaks under cover when it is heaviest.
- Give instructions with the students' backs to the wind. This means that they are more comfortable, and, if in a tight circle, they will help protect you.
- Have a light tarpaulin under which the group can take shelter for a few minutes of respite, to receive instructions or discuss plans.
- Use the lee of topographical features (hollows, tree lines) and physical features (building walls) as conditions dictate. These can be incorporated as stations into your lesson plans.

Temperature

Broadly speaking, there are two ways to raise a person's low body temperature. The first and most desirable way is to ensure that they are generating their own heat by moving. In most cases, even if one is reasonably dressed for the conditions, staying still for half an hour outside will lead to feeling cold. Therefore, it is important to remain active.

The second way to raise a person's temperature is to do it for them through insulation and external warming. This is more of an emergency procedure, as it means that the cold person is so hypothermic that they are not able to move by themselves and generate their own heat. Teachers should monitor their students as a matter of course and any decline in cognitive and motor function will be very obvious if a person is becoming hypothermic.[1]

Teaching tips

- Have a stock of quick, fun, active games up your sleeve. These can effectively warm up and energize young bodies and minds.[2]
- In colder climes, in particular, have a ready supply of healthy snacks to help guard against children getting cold.

---

1 People whose body temperature is significantly dropping will exhibit 'the umbles' – mumbles, stumbles, fumbles, etc.
2 See for example the range of activities that can be found in classic Project Adventure books, such as QuickSilver, Silver Bullets, Cowstails, and Cobras II.

Many schools and education districts will have guidance regarding the ways in which specific environmental conditions may limit outdoor activity. For example, guidance on increased air pollution, high winds, hot/cold temperatures, lightning, prolonged snow-fall, and widespread ice levels may be cited in policy documents. This local guidance should generally be followed, unless it is over-taken by a specific or dynamic risk-assessment.

External factors: traffic, water features, distracting events

Everything in the 'external factors' category refers to non-environmental and non-human factors that need managing. If we are giving instructions on the sidewalk and a street-cleaning machine comes by or a protest march appears from around the corner, what can be done? If a friendly dog comes into the middle of our circle while we are talking, how can it be ignored? What about an aggressive dog?!

Unforeseen events often rely on teachers improvising and 'thinking on their feet'. As discussed in Chapter 8, it is impossible to plan for every conceivable risk. If hazards present themselves, then you are expected to act swiftly and reasonably.

Teaching tips

- If you expect there might be some distractions from your lesson outside the classroom, then it may be best to give instructions or have group discussions either back in the classroom (before and after) or to retreat to a quieter, less distracting area for these occasions.
- Before venturing outside, discuss with your students the distractions that may present themselves, and how these will be dealt with. For example, if a plane is flying low overhead, teaching will pause until the noise has abated.

Human factors: managing primary needs and group dynamics

Beyond addressing individual primary needs by ensuring that students are adequately fed and watered and suitably clothed, teachers have to manage group behaviour and attend to specific individual needs and dispositions. It may be prudent to discuss with students the appropriate behaviour for, say, walking from one place to another, negotiating a hazard (e.g. crossing a road), or being in a public building.

Teachers know their students and know their surroundings and so should be able to foresee many of the events that might influence group dynamics or trigger certain behaviours. By planning ahead as much as possible and by identifying the environmental, external, and human factors that could present themselves, teachers will be more able to manage risks and distractions during outings.

Teaching tips

- When necessary, maintain concentration and attention levels by highlighting student responsibilities and agreed codes of behaviour.
- Ensure that disruptive students are supervised closely and remain 'grounded' throughout the lesson – especially when arousal levels increase.

THE QUESTION OF RATIOS

Many teachers seem to want definitive guidance on ratios. Schools and regions will have their own specific guidance on adult/student ratios. Teachers need to be aware of any prescribed ratios and incorporate them into their planning. Certainly, in most cases within the school grounds, one teacher should be able to manage a class on their own. Once away from the school, having two responsible, capable adults accompanying would be considered the minimum. Should any incident need managing, one adult can deal with this, while the other manages the group. Although having a third adult can be seen as a relative luxury, it does mean that in the event of a child not feeling well and having to return to school with one adult (for example), the lesson can continue as planned, as two adults remain to maintain an accepted ratio for uncomplicated learning outside the classroom.

Generally, policy guidance uses terms such as 'suitable ratios' of adults to participants. Obviously, this is incredibly vague, as whatever is 'suitable' will depend on:

- the age and ability of the group;
- the 'reliability' of the group;

- the number of students with additional support or medical needs;
- the nature of the activities/outing;
- the supervising adults' experience in leading groups off-site;
- the nature of the site, and whether this is a fixed location (e.g. a park) or whether the activities involve moving locations.

While most of these bullet points will be obvious to any teacher, the last item – 'site' – is worthy of special mention in relation to ratios in particular. Nicolazzo (2007) explains that sites, in their most basic sense, can be seen as stationary or moving. Stationary sites (e.g. the garden at the town hall) are generally considered much safer than moving sites (e.g. walking to the town hall), as the 'hazards and safe zones are known prior to the activity' (p. 26). With moving sites, which involve the group travelling from one place to another, not all of the hazards may be known until they are encountered.

Nicolazzo (2007) stresses that since boundaries are fixed and the hazards can be seen in stationary sites, this is where all teaching should take place. If a group was walking from one place to another and the teacher wanted the group to stop and discuss a certain phenomenon (e.g. the architecture of a building), the most prudent course of action would be to turn this situation into a stationary site, by ensuring that the group was in a 'safe zone' within clearly delineated boundaries.

Having one extra adult will often make the ratios more manageable for most low-risk, local outings. Naturally, advice from the school district or local council must be followed. As discussed in the risk management chapter, much of your decision-making will come down to 'what a reasonable and prudent person would do' in the same circumstances. The result of careful planning and taking advice from others should be a ratio of adults to children that is appropriate for your unique set of circumstances. Teachers are used to judging appropriate ratios and arranging for suitable supervision. The move out of the school building requires adjusting these common practices.

MANAGING THE GROUP *EN ROUTE*

As mentioned above, there is no 'best' way to travel together through a park or on the sidewalk – only the most appropriate. However, there are a number of vital elements that should be considered.

First, ensure that you, as teacher, are carrying a class list of all participants and adults at all times. Counting the number of students before, as often as needed during the outing, and afterwards will be a matter of course. Keeping track of students during outings can take two broad approaches: students checking on students (e.g. 'wingers') and adults checking on students (e.g. with class or pod list). For student/student checks, threes can work particularly well. An example of this is the 'winger' system, where students make a circle at the start of the outing so that each person has a 'buddy' on either side of them. At any time during an outing, a teacher can ask everyone to confirm that their winger is present.

In terms of how the class travels, there are many variations; each has its own merits. Generally speaking, classes can travel as one big group that moves as a 'blob', in pairs, with wingers, or with independent pods of students. With the latter, each pod of five to nine students will travel with its own responsible, vetted (because they are working independently) adult. Creative student/student and adult/student check-in systems can be developed for pods and large classes alike. There is no doubt, however, that a class divided into two to four pods (rather than one big class) can rapidly check on students being present and address pressing primary needs. Certainly, students should know who is their adult supervisor.

Consider having your students wear identifiable apparel (e.g. vests, hats, shirts). This may be more appropriate in some contexts than others (e.g. urban settings). As part of the boundaries briefing, children should be briefed on what to do (or where to meet) should they become separated from the class. In some circumstances (e.g. very crowded urban settings), it is worth considering giving participants badges with the name of the establishment and its emergency contact number.

In some instances with reliable and relatively experienced groups, more freedom and less close supervision may be appropriate. Suitable circumstances may present themselves in government buildings and parks, for example. In these scenarios, teachers will need to ensure that:

- this is an appropriate decision, based on learning outcomes and the group having a reasonable 'reliability record' when learning outside the class-room;
- appropriate boundaries have been outlined;
- hazards that are likely to be encountered are highlighted by the students;
- students have been divided into suitable pods/work groups and that these are recorded by the teacher;
- they have established a system where they can regularly verify that everyone is accounted for;
- students have been briefed on what do in the event of an emergency (e.g. Who do they call or notify? Where is the meeting point? Where will the teacher and other adults be?).

In most learning outside the classroom circumstances there will be one dedicated cellphone that one student or adult will carry on behalf of the group. However, in less-close supervision scenarios, each pod will need to have their own phone.

TEACHING AND SHARING INFORMATION OUTDOORS

What is the best way to teach a concept or share information with a group? Watch any seasoned teacher working outdoors and you'll probably see most of the discussion happening in circles. With circles, everyone gets to be in the 'front row'; students' possibilities to listen, see, and speak can be greatly increased. A rounded horseshoe shape can also be used if more of a stage or 'front-of-the-class' is required. Lines, too, can be useful for drawing attention to one point of reference, just as huddles are effective for quickly sharing brief pieces of information. Obviously, a range of strategies exist for sharing information with others and the most appropriate option will depend on what it is the teacher is trying to achieve in a given location, with fluid external, environmental, and human factors.

As noted above, in sunny settings, wherever possible ensure that students are not facing the sun. As the teacher, organizing a horseshoe with you at the open top facing the sun is best for students. Of course, under the circumstances, you may feel the need to wear sunglasses. However, this will mean losing crucial eye contact with your students (unless you are using orange or rose coloured glasses, as mentioned above). In windy settings, consider gathering the group in a tight circle through which little air can pass. The teacher can face into the wind if he/she is being sufficiently protected by a tight bunch of surrounding bodies.

Cooperative learning strategies also have their place when disseminating information or instructions (see Chapters 6 and 7). Teachers can brief a small group of messengers, who can then go and share information with their peers – also in small circles.

Remember that all teaching should be done at a stationary site, where there are clear boundaries and all of the hazards are identified and managed.

CROSSING ROADS

Anything to do with students and road traffic can be considered higher risk. As crossing roads is something that people do frequently throughout their lifetimes, it is justifiable to do it on a class outing, if it is run as an activity with an educational aim.

Wherever possible, roads should be crossed at a designated pedestrian crossing – whether one with lights or a simple zebra crossing. Drawing from the above site management terms, road crossings should be considered stationary sites. Even though crossing the road is part of a larger journey, the actual crossing is turned into a mini-activity in itself. In practice, this means three things. First, boundaries will be fixed (on the original side of the road, the other side, and of course, for the actual crossing). Second, instructions will be given regarding when to cross, what to do (where to wait) on the other side, and perhaps how to travel (e.g. alone, with a buddy, in a pod). Third, teachers will need to decide on the most appropriate location for them to be placed, should they need to intervene for educational/instructional or safety reasons.

In rural areas, with no designated pedestrian crossings, and less frequent traffic, a different approach to group crossings may be considered. Rather than travel in a line that cuts across the flow of traffic (as one would at a cross-walk), it may be appropriate to cross as one group, parallel to the direction of traffic. First, students organize themselves into one long line of people standing by the side of the road. Teachers placed at each end of the line, being the eyes and ears, can give each other the 'all clear' signal, in which case the group crosses the road at the same speed. This way, an on-coming car (that could not be seen or heard before the crossing started) will not come upon a road full of people – only the 'area' of one person. This allows the drivers to adjust their course, as there is plenty of open road on which to do so.

VOLUNTEERS, PARENTS, AND ADULT ASSISTANTS

Parents and adult volunteers are an effective way to increase adult to student ratios. It may be that those who have not been vetted are not allowed to be left in sole charge of students. It is generally not necessary to arrange 'checks' for both adult helpers and those in the community working with students, who will have only limited contact with students (see Chapter 8). Volunteers who are going to be in substantial or regular contact with students may be required to undergo a check and follow the school's (or education district's) specific volunteer protocol.

Care must be taken to arrange appropriate supervision for activities where changing clothes is necessary (e.g. sports and swimming) and personal assistance for children with additional support needs is required. While these events are often planned far in advance, impromptu learning sessions outside the classroom (by their very nature) are not. So, outdoor learning sessions that take place off-campus may be more difficult to organize on a spontaneous level.

Adult volunteers can be made even more useful if they have specific roles. These roles may have to do with the emergency action plan, with crossing roads, or with paying extra attention to particular students with specific needs.

TOILETING, PERSONAL PRIVACY, AND HYGIENE

Perhaps one of the trickiest issues to deal with when learning outside the classroom is going to the toilet. Even if everyone urinates before a short outing, there is always the possibility that someone will need to go again once out and about. In these cases, areas with trees may lend themselves more readily to providing some personal privacy. Consider referring to guidelines on human waste that are appropriate to the ecosystem in which you live. Unless the outing is an extended one, if the children do need to relieve themselves, it will usually be to urinate. Most boys will be fine with this (e.g. behind a tree). Privacy, and perhaps the unfamiliarity of urinating outside, may be issues for girls, however. Girls may need to go out of sight in twos or threes with a female leader. Keep in mind that adults in the group need a system in place for when they need to go as well!

In more urban centres, where outdoor privacy cannot be found and a public toilet is the most suitable option, circumstances can become more difficult to manage, as there may be lots of other people around. As with road crossings, one effective management tool is to turn the toilet break into an activity; and activities need to be regarded as stationary sites.

First, boundaries are fixed and the group not using the toilet is 'parked' in a designated area. Second, instructions are given regarding for waiting with the group, travelling to and from the toilet, and being inside the actual toilet. Third, teachers will need to decide where to place themselves: with the group, *en route* (if the main group is parked a little bit away from the toilet) or at the toilet. The teacher monitoring the toilet can be outside, or in the case of a large public toilet (where two or more students are going) they can supervise from the inside.

Teachers will have their own systems for managing toilet use in the school or on field trips. Perhaps most importantly, they will know their students' individual needs. These factors are perhaps more useful than generic guidance found in a book!

Eating and drinking is generally straightforward, in terms of managing hygiene. Students will have their own water bottles and often their own snacks. Irrespective of where food comes from, ensure effective hand hygiene practices are undertaken before eating. As an absolute minimum, it is good practice to wash hands after using the toilet, before eating and preparing food, and of

103

course, any time one's hands are soiled. We recommend following school guidance, and World Health Organization (2009) guidelines that are available on their website.

THE 'OFF-SITE' KIT

Having an 'off-site' kit ready to go makes regular and spontaneous learning outside the classroom much more feasible. This kit can be managed (to a degree) by the class, and its contents kept in a backpack and file-folder. It may consist of:

- a generic risk assessment for local outings and the emergency action plan;
- student and staff information (medical information, next of kin contact details);
- a hazardous waste kit (including 'tuff' gloves and a box for picking up glass/sharps and gloves/bags for picking up dog feces);
- hand wipes and/or anti-bacterial hand wash (or similar);
- a first aid kit;
- blank journey plans and hazard assessments for students to complete before leaving;
- extra warm layers/hats.

CASE STUDY

Every Wednesday morning, Kay's grade 4 class walks to a local park about 20 minutes away. The journey is partly on a disused railway line and partly the sidewalk of a busy road. Naturally, Kay and her assistant have developed a thorough risk management strategy that is kept in the school's main office.

In her off-site kit, Kay has the students' blanket consent forms (with their parent/carer contact information), a first aid kit with any specific medications that are used by students, extra food and drink (this could be carried by students), appropriate spare clothing, and possibly a very lightweight shelter.

On her way to school on Wednesday mornings, Kay habitually goes to the site and makes sure that there are no obvious unforeseen hazards present. She then goes in to work via the same route that the students will take that day.

Before leaving the school for the site, Lauren and Mike (both students) have taken a copy of the class journey plan to the office. This document outlines who is going where and when, what they took, their designated cell phone number, and their estimated time of return. Lauren and Mike had filled in the blank template at the end of the previous day.

It's very windy and is raining slightly, and everyone except for two boys has a decent waterproof jacket to wear. Kay gives them two old yellow rain jackets that were donated to the school a couple of years back.

The first site of the day is a moving one, where the group travels *en masse* along the former railway line. Kay is at the rear, while her two assistants are in the middle and at the front. Once they get to the road, the group knows that it's time to get into their pre-arranged walking pairs, as per their briefing in the class. This allows them to walk on the sidewalk in an orderly fashion, while leaving enough room for other pedestrians to pass.

When they get to the zebra crossing, Kay's teaching assistant (Scott) and a parent volunteer (Leslie) wait until the traffic stops for them. They then cross to the middle of the zebra crossing, and signal for the pairs to walk across. Kay crosses last.

When the group arrives at the stationary site, but before entering, Kay and two students quickly check the area for dog feces, branches that have broken off and could fall, and anything else that could be harmful. During these few minutes, Scott and Leslie ensure that everyone has a small drink and snack and suggest that people put on or take off a layer of clothing if they need to. Kay and the students return from their 'reconnaissance mission' and report to the group that the site poses no obvious risks.

At this point, before beginning the activity, Kay surveys the group to see how they are doing in terms of being adequately fed, hydrated, and warm. She notices that since they stopped walking, the wind has also picked up. Kay makes a mental note to ensure that the students get active as soon as possible so they will keep warm. She keeps a special eye on the temperature for the rest of the morning and considers how she can help the students stay warm through various parts of the lesson.

In order to contend with the range of human, environmental, and external factors that might be encountered, teachers' abilities to adapt to these constantly changing circumstances are of paramount importance. Having this 'big picture' overview and managing its fluid nature has been called a *meta-skill* (Priest & Gass, 1997), and refers to a teacher's ability to make decisions, solve problems, and use their judgment.

So, this ability to 'think on one's feet' and respond to ever-changing conditions can be seen as a vital component of supervising other people outdoors. As Barton (2007) notes, teachers who don't use their common sense and judgment fail to do so at their peril. If, while on an outing, conditions and circumstances have changed, teachers must not hesitate to alter their plans in order to reduce the likelihood of encountering certain hazards.

The skills and experience to teach outside the classroom are not 'dark arts' that only a few special people possess. They are tools that can be gradually developed over time. The key, we suggest, is starting small, staying close to home, being alert to changing circumstances, and keeping initial outings manageable.

GUIDELINES

- When teaching in the outdoors, teachers need to address environmental, human, and external factors that may distract, and possibly harm, students. These three broad factors will need to be addressed before delivering instructions or educational content.
- Activities outside the school take place in sites that can be thought of as either stationary or moving. Stationary sites are generally much safer and are best for sharing information. Careful instructions about expectations and boundaries are vital to managing sites.
- Classes can travel together as one group, together in twos and threes, or separated into smaller independent 'pods' – each of which is managed by a responsible, vetted adult.
- Keeping track of students during outings can be in two different ways: students checking on students (e.g. 'wingers'/'buddies') and adults checking on students (e.g. going through the whole roll or each adult checking on their pod of eight students).
- A pre-prepared off-site kit will enable more spontaneous excursions outside the classroom.

Chapter 10

Putting it all together

Developing an action plan to take learning outdoors

CHAPTER AIMS

- Understand three initial steps that can be taken to lay the foundation for taking class learning outside the classroom.
- Be aware of four additional, place-based strategies that can be considered when choosing the most appropriate approach to learning outside the classroom.
- Encourage teachers to take their first steps towards becoming as competent and comfortable when teaching outdoors as they are indoors.
- Re-emphasize that there is a world of learning opportunities beyond the classroom door.

HOW CAN THE FIRST NINE CHAPTERS BE PUT TOGETHER?

Many teachers are over-worked and, quite rightly, see changes to learning content and approaches to delivery as an additional burden on their limited time. We acknowledge that moving from ways of teaching that have been traditionally indoors, tightly constrained, and highly prescribed towards teaching that integrates the outdoors and is multi-disciplinary, can be challenging, to say the least!

Although the first nine chapters of the book are presented in a way that is intended to be 'joined up', it can of course be daunting to try to put all of this into practice at once. But you don't have to! Ways of incorporating themes of place, sustainability, community, and responsibility into teaching and learning can be gradual. In many cases it wouldn't be possible to incorporate all of the themes at once, and in some cases it might not be appropriate. This transition towards teaching outside the classroom is best done by degree, rather than by sweeping wholescale changes; a slower progression will be more natural for students, teachers, administrators, and parents.

Even if you are keen to adapt your curriculum so that it is 'clearly grounded in local issues and possibilities' (Smith & Sobel, 2010, p. 57), these changes do not have to happen overnight. Rather than attempting to 'tick all the boxes', which may actually limit students' depth of inquiry into an area of study, we suggest you start by making a deliberate plan to incorporate two or three of the themes (e.g. cross-curricular learning and sustainability) as you see fit.

So, while working on a gardening project in the school grounds may be in keeping with much of the book's content, without interacting with others in the community and without serving others in the community it would not technically be 'community-based'. This is okay! Just because it doesn't incorporate every single guideline doesn't mean that it is not a valuable and worthy project that will yield all kinds of opportunities to learn. The trick is being creative and imaginative enough to give students the power and resources to learn across the curriculum in ways that also incorporate three elements that have universal and cross-cultural significance: literacy, numeracy, and health and well-being.

FIRST STEPS: RISK MANAGEMENT

Do a generic risk assessment and emergency action plan for school grounds and local outdoor learning sessions. These should include public transport and be done in keeping with your school's health and safety policies. These two items will need to be checked by someone in a position of authority, such as your principal or a health and safety specialist from the district – one of whom should be able to support and advise you throughout this process. If you are unfamiliar with this process or feel daunted by it, try enlisting the support of a more experienced colleague in the school. Alternatively, there may be an outdoor learning specialist in your area who might be able to help.

Compose a blanket consent form. This will be signed by students' parents/guardians and kept on file. Being able to do spontaneous, frequent outdoor learning depends greatly on having this form. As above, seek knowledgeable support in order to ensure that this form is sufficiently comprehensive. Unfortunately, some schools and districts have local regulations that prevent the use of 'blanket' forms.

Put together an 'off-site kit' for learning outdoors. This kit includes the above administration, blank hazard assessments and journey plans (to be filled out by students), group gear, individual items of clothing (e.g. a spare warm jacket), and a first aid kit. Obviously, this will be altered in order to fit various climates by, for example, substituting cold weather gear for sun screen and brimmed hats.

Although all of the above may seem like a lot of work, keep in mind that these tasks need to be done only once, at the beginning of the year. Indeed, even the year after, it will be a matter of tweaking your systems, rather than writing and organizing them from scratch. As highlighted in Chapter 6, students should be taking some responsibility to help you with this. A team approach ensures that you are not left doing all the work, and are not faced with explaining 'your rules' to the children; they know what to expect and what is expected of them when they go outdoors. Crucially, planning for outings becomes part of the curriculum (as opposed to something you have to do after school on your own time).

SECOND STEPS: PLACE-BASED LEARNING

Once the important safety and logistical elements have been put in place, we can turn our attention to more germane aspects of learning through local landscape in relation to the curriculum you intend to deliver. At this point we can revisit Smith and Sobel's (2010) four categories of place and community-based education: nature, culture, enterprise, and citizenship.

Consider which categories will be most easily used as a means of bringing your curriculum outdoors. The particular landscape in which the school is located, the opportunities and 'needs' of the local neighbourhood, and the interests of the students will all influence the shape of your class's outdoor learning.

Construct a list of possible individual and organization partners who might be able to help you broaden the delivery of your students' curriculum. These people might play a supporting logistical role, such a parent who can offer an extra set of hands and eyes. Other partners can be found within local businesses, charities, voluntary organizations, and government services. Examples of these could be a nearby bakery, the councillor's office, a conservation society, or the municipal park service.

Identify obvious links between specific intended learning outcomes within the curriculum and the surrounding physical environment and local issues. Outcomes relating to the 'big three' of literacy, numeracy, and health and well-being can be linked to most learning outside the classroom ventures.

Secondary school teachers who are teaching specific subject areas, such as art, physics, or geography, may find it more natural to identify particular elements of the curriculum that are especially suited to learning in a more authentic setting than a classroom. As discussed in Chapter 2, teachers are encouraged to teach across disciplines. In some secondary school contexts this may be facilitated (where timetables permit) by teachers 'joining forces' to deliver two subject areas over a double period.

Find and work with a mentor who has experience of taking their class outdoors as part of an integrated approach to delivering the curriculum. If nearby support is not available, there is an increasing number of teachers who are discussing teaching practice and sharing ideas online.[1]

The above items can be seen as subjects of ongoing discussion with peers, mentors, parents, partners, and, of course, students.

GUIDELINES

- First, take care of three steps for managing risk:
  - Conduct a risk assessment and emergency action plan for outdoor learning in the school grounds and local area (e.g. within two miles of the school).
  - Write a blanket consent form that will inform parents and carers about your plans while securing their permission for you to take their child outside for class throughout the year.
  - Prepare an off-site kit that contains the necessary paper work and equipment for you to take learning outside the classroom as spontaneously as possible.

- Second, consider four strategies for fostering place-based learning:
  - Consider which categories of place- and community-based outdoor learning (nature, culture, enterprise, citizenship) may initially lend themselves to the unique circumstances of your place and its people.
  - Identify individuals and organizations within the community who may be able to act as allies and co-educators.
  - Identify obvious intended learning outcomes within the curriculum that you are expected to deliver.

1 Children and Nature Connect is an international forum that connects teachers, parents, and outdoor practitioners. See http://childrenandnature.ning.com/

— Find and work with a mentor who has experience of taking a class outdoors.

TAKING THE PLUNGE . . .

Smith (2002) captures many of our beliefs regarding the way contemporary education needs to become. He notes that 'Teachers must become the creators of curriculum rather than the dispensers of curriculum developed by others' (p. 593). Creating a curriculum, however, may be neither possible (due to district, state, or national regulations) nor feasible (since it will be a huge amount of work).

What we can do is bring much of the formal curriculum alive by taking students into the school grounds and local neighbourhood. If we are teaching students to succeed in exams, then the classroom and exam hall are authentic contexts in which to learn. However, if we want our students to possess personally useful knowledge from across the curriculum, to be meaningfully engaged in community life, and to live sustainably on their land, then the authentic learning context must include the world in which they live and go to school.

Integrating outdoor and indoor teaching capitalizes on children's natural curiosity about the people and places encountered in their everyday lives. In an age when our children desperately need the biological, cognitive, and spiritual benefits associated with 'positive physical connection to nature' (Louv, 2008, p. 36), how can teachers, parents, and policy-makers accept that most (if not all) formal education has to take place in a classroom?

While all this guidance and so many things to remember might seem daunting, always remember that *you are the expert*, in terms of knowing your curriculum, your 'place', and, most importantly, your students. Crossing the threshold does indeed take a certain amount of confidence, but our experience working with teachers indicates that the majority of their fears melt away once they are actually outdoors! After all, this is experiential learning we are talking about, and one can't imagine away these fears theoretically. However, with experience fears do ease, and they are replaced by an emotion that is not based on fear or anxiety, but on opportunities for learning and growth.

Confucius is reported to have said that 'a journey of a thousand miles begins with a single step'. By reading this book, you have now taken your first step in finding out the basic 'whys' and 'hows' of learning outside the classroom. The next step is to venture outdoors with your students and experience the possibilities for yourselves (and we acknowledge that many who read this book already do so). Let us not underestimate the significance of these first steps, because the stakes are high. Our planet's environment, and our social and economic systems will experience dramatic changes in the twenty-first century, and today's students will become the adults who encounter these changes. Facing these on a personal and professional level will require a clear understanding of our interdependence as individuals and communities with our planet, its resources, and biodiversity. To encounter this as reality requires venturing outside the classroom.

As teachers, our highest ambition is to pass on a lasting positive legacy to our students – to help them develop the knowledge, attributes, and skills required to address these complex issues; and this is simply not possible if our teaching is entirely indoors. We do not believe that outdoor learning is the sole solution to addressing these complex issues, but we do believe it can help, because there is something special – perhaps even magical – to be found in the outdoors. These learning experiences can make a lasting difference to young people's lives – they certainly did to ours!

As we stated at the end of the preface, this book is not just about outdoor learning; it's about good teaching – wherever it takes place. It's about helping teachers devise and use the tools with which they can address the largely uncontested assumption that legitimate learning only occurs within four walls. Learning outside the classroom affords us the privilege of helping, and the joy of observing, students in a process of intellectual, emotional, and social growth that can last a lifetime.

References

Arnone, M. (2003). *Using instructional design strategies to foster curiosity.* ERIC Digest: ED479842. Source: ERIC Clearinghouse on Information & Technology.

Atkinson, R., Smith, E., Bem, D., & Hoeksema, S. (1993). *Hargard's introduction to psychology* (12th ed). Fort Worth, TX: Harcourt Brace Jovanovich.

Backman, E. (2010). *Friluftsliv in Swedish physical education – a struggle of values: Educational and sociological perspectives.* Unpublished PhD thesis, Stockholm University.

Baker, M. (2005). Landfullness in adventure-based programming: Promoting reconnection to the land. *Journal of Experiential Education, 27*(3), 267–276.

Barone, T. (2000). *Aesthetics, politics, and educational inquiry.* New York: Peter Lang.

Barton, B. (2007). *Safety, risk, and adventure in outdoor activities.* London: Sage.

Beames, S. (2006). Losing my religion: The struggle to find applicable theory. *Pathways: The Ontario Journal of Outdoor Education, 19*(1), 4–11.

Beames, S., & Atencio, M. (2008). Building social capital through outdoor education. *Journal of Adventure Education & Outdoor Learning, 8*(2), 99–112.

Beames, S., & Ross, H. (2010). Journeys outside the classroom. *Journal of Adventure Education & Outdoor Learning, 10*(2), 95-109.

Beames, S., Atencio, M., & Ross, H. (2009). Taking excellence outdoors. *Scottish Educational Review, 41*(2) 32–45.

Bee, H. (1989). *The developing child* (5th ed). New York: Harper & Row.

Bell, S., Hamilton, V., Montarzino, A., Rothnie, H., Travlou, P., & Alves, S. (2008). *Greenspace and quality of life: A critical literature review.* Stirling: Greenspace Scotland.

Bentsen, P., Mygind, E., & Randrup, T.B. (2009). Towards an understanding of udeskole: Education outside the classroom in a Danish context. *Education 3–13, 37*(1), 29–44.

Berlyne, D.E. (1960). *Conflict, arousal, and curiosity.* New York: McGraw Hill.

REFERENCES

Bilton, H. (2010). *Outdoor learning in the early years: Management and innovation*. London: Routledge/Taylor Francis Group.

Bird, W. (2007). *Natural thinking*. Retrieved from http://www.rspb.org.uk/Images/natural thinking_tcm9-161856.pdf

Blair, D. (2009). The child in the garden: An evaluative review of the benefits of school gardening. *Journal of Environmental Education, 40*(2), 15–38.

Blank, M., & Berg, A. (2006). *All together now: Sharing responsibility for the whole child*. Washington, DC: Coalition for Community Schools.

Boud, D., Cohen, R., & Walker, D. (1993). *Using experience for learning*. Buckingham: Open University Press.

Brody, C., & Davidson, N. (1998). Introduction: Professional development and cooperative learning. In C. Brody & N. Davidson (Eds), *Professional development for cooperative learning: Issues and approaches* (pp. 3–24). Albany, NY: SUNY Press.

Brookes, A. (2002). Lost in the Australian bush: Outdoor education as curriculum. *Journal of Curriculum Studies, 34*(4), 405–425.

Butin, D.W. (2010). *Service-learning in theory and practice: The future of community engagement in higher education*. New York: Palgrave Macmillan.

Chawla, L. (1998). Significant life experiences revisited: A review of research on sources of environmental sensitivity. *Journal of Environmental Education, 29*(3), 11–21.

CLOC (Council for Learning Outside the Classroom). (2006). *Manifesto for learning outside the classroom*. Retrieved from http://www.lotc.org.uk

Cook, L. (1999). The 1944 education act and outdoor education: From policy to practice. *History of Education, 28*(2), 157–172.

Curriculum Review Group. (2007). *A curriculum for excellence*. Retrieved from http://www.scotland.gov.uk/Publications/2004/11/20178/45862

Danks, F., & Schofield, J. (2005). Nature's playground. London: Francis Lincoln.

Dawson, P., & Guare, R. (2010). *Executive skills in children and adolescents: A practical guide to assessment and intervention* (2nd ed). New York: The Guildford Press.

Day, H.I. (1982). Curiosity and the interested explorer. *NSPI Journal*, May, 19–22.

Department for Education and Skills. (2006). *Learning outside the classroom manifesto*. Nottingham: DfES.

Dewey, J. (1973). Experience is pedagogical. In J.J. McDermott (Ed), *The philosophy of John Dewey* (pp. 421–523). Chicago: The University of Chicago Press.

Donaldson, M. (1978). *Children's minds*. London: Fontana Press.

Dymoke, S., & Harrison, J. (2008). *Reflective teaching and learning*. London: Sage.

Earth Charter Initiative. (2000). *The Earth Charter*. Retrieved from http://web.archive.org/web/20071012234735/www.earthcharterinaction.org/2000/10/the_earth_charter.html

Eisner, E. (1985). The three curricula that all schools teach. In E. Eisner (Ed), *The educational imagination* (pp. 87–108). New York: Macmillan.

Fjørtoft, I. (2004). Landscape as playscape: The effects of natural environments on children's play and motor development. *Children, Youth and Environments, 14*(2), 21–44.

Foxfire. (n.d.). *Foxfire*. Retrieved from http://www.foxfire.org/articles/FoxfireFundInc.pdf

Freire, P. (1972). *Pedagogy of the oppressed*. Harmondsworth: Penguin.

Furedi, F. (2002). *Culture of fear*. London: Cassell.

Furedi, F. (2009). Precautionary culture and the rise of possibilistic risk assessment. *Erasmus Law Review, 2*(2), 197–220.

Furedi, F., & Bristow, H. (2008). *Licensed to hug: How child protection policies are poisoning the relationship between the generations and damaging the voluntary sector.* London: Civitas.

Gardner, H. (1993). *Frames of mind: The theory of multiple intelligences* (2nd ed). London: Fontana.

Gatto, J.T. (2005). *Dumbing us down: The hidden curriculum of compulsory schooling.* Gabriola Island, BC: New Society.

Gill, T. (2007). *No fear: Growing up in a risk averse society.* London: Calouste Gulbenkian Foundation.

Gill, T. (2010). *Nothing ventured: Balancing risks and benefits in the outdoors.* England: English Outdoor Council.

Ginsburg, H., & Opper S. (1969). *Piaget's theory of intellectual development: An introduction.* New Jersey: Prentice Hall.

Giroux, H., & Penna, A. (1983). Social education in the classroom: The dynamics of the hidden curriculum. In H. Giroux, & D. Purpel (Eds), *The hidden curriculum and moral education: Deception or discovery?* (pp. 100–121). Berkeley: McCutchan.

Glover, D., & Law, S. (2002). *Improving learning: Professional practice in secondary schools.* Buckingham: Open University Press.

Goddard Blythe, S. (2004). *The well balanced child: Movement and early learning.* Stroud: Hawthorn Press.

Gregg, C. (n.d.). *Ideology.* Retrieved from http://www.rebgregg.com/ideology/index.php

Gregg, C. (2005). Managing the risks of a lawsuit. In D. Ajango (Ed.), *Lessons learned II: Using case studies and history to improve safety education* (pp. 181–207). Palm Springs, CA: Watchmaker.

Harrison, S. (2010). 'Why are we here?': Taking place into account in UK outdoor environmental education. *Journal of Adventure Education and Outdoor Learning, 10*(1), 1–16.

Health and Safety Executive. (2007). *We are about saving lives, not stopping living!* Retrieved from http://www.hse.gov.uk/press/2007/e07010.htm

Henderson, B. (2010). Understanding heritage travel: Story, place, and technology. In S. Beames (Ed.), *Understanding educational expeditions* (pp. 79–89). Rotterdam: Sense.

Henderson, B., & Vikander, N. (Eds) (2007). *Nature first: Outdoor life the friluftsliv way.* Toronto: Natural Heritage Books.

Higgins, P. (2009). Into the big wide world: Sustainable experiential education for the 21st century. *Journal of Experiential Education, 32*(1), 44–60.

Higgins, P. (2010). Pedagogy for 'global intimacy'. In T. Wiseley, I. Barr, & B. King (Eds), *Education in a global space: Research and practice in initial teacher education* (pp. 180–188). Edinburgh: International Development Education Association of Scotland and Scotdec.

Higgins, P., & Nicol, R. (Eds) (2002). *Outdoor education: Authentic learning through landscapes* (Vol. 2). Sweden: Kinda Kunskapscentrum. Retrieved from http://www.education.ed.ac.uk/outdoored/resources.html

REFERENCES

Higgins, P., & Nicol, R. (Eds) (2002). *Outdoor education: Authentic learning through landscapes (Vol. 2)*. An international collaboration project supported by the European Union Comenius Action 2. European In-Service Training Courses.

Higgins, P., & Nicol, R. (2011). Professor Sir Patrick Geddes: *'Vivendo Discimus'* – by living we learn. In C. Knapp, & T. Smith (Eds), *A sourcebook for experiential education: Key thinkers and their contributions* (pp. 32–40). New York: Routledge.

Higgins, P., Nicol, R., & Ross, H. (2006). *Teachers' approaches and attitudes to engaging with the natural heritage through the curriculum*. Perth: Scottish Natural Heritage.

Hopkins, D., & Putnam, R. (1993). *Personal growth through adventure*. Bristol: Taylor & Francis.

Hurlock, E.B. (1978). *Child development*. London: McGraw-Hill.

Ife, J. (2002). *Community development*. Frenchs Forest, Australia: Pearson Education.

Ife, J. (2010). *Human rights from below: Achieving rights through community development*. Cambridge: Cambridge University Press.

Illich, I. (1996). *Deschooling society*. London: Marion Boyars.

IPCC (Intergovernmental Panel on Climate Change). (2007). Fourth Assessment Report. (AR 4 Climate Change 2007). Retrieved from http://www.ipcc.ch/. Melbourne: Australian International Press and Publications.

IUCN (International Union for the Conservation of Nature and Natural Resources). (1980). *World conservation strategy: Living resource conservation for sustainable development*. Gland, Switzerland: IUCN.

Johnson, D.W., & Johnson, R.T. (1999). Learning together. In S. Sharan (Ed.), *Cooperative learning methods* (pp. 51–65). Westport, CT: Praeger.

Jolliffe, W. (2007). *Cooperative learning in the classroom: Putting it into practice*. London: Paul Chapman.

Kelly, A.V. (2009). *The curriculum: Theory and practice*. London: Sage.

Kibble, R. (2010). *Sunshine, shadows and stone circles*. Sandbach, UK: Millgate House.

Learning and Teaching Scotland. (2010). *Curriculum for excellence through outdoor learning*. Glasgow: Learning & Teaching Scotland. Retrieved from http://www.ltscotland.org.uk/outdoorlearning/curriculumforexcellence/index.asp

Leopold, A. (1966). *A Sand County Almanac with essays on conservation from Round River*. New York: Oxford University Press.

Loewenstein, G. (1994). The psychology of curiosity: A review and reinterpretation. *The Psychology Bulletin, 116*(1), 75–98.

Louv, R. (2008). *Last child in the woods: Saving our children from nature-deficit disorder*. New York: Algonquin Books.

Lucas, A. (1979). *Environment and environmental education: Conceptual issues and curriculum implications*. Melbourne: Australian International Press & Publications.

Maeda, K. (2005). Community-based outdoor education using a local approach to conservation. *Australian Journal of Outdoor Education, 9*(1), 40–47.

Martin, P. (2008). Teacher qualification guidelines, ecological literacy and outdoor education. *Australian Journal of Outdoor Education, 12*(2), 32–38.

Martin, P. (2010). Outdoor education and the national curriculum in Australia. *Australian Journal of Outdoor Education, 14*(2), 3–11.

Martin, B., Cashel, C., Wagstaff, M., and Breunig, M. (2006). *Outdoor leadership: Theory and practice*. Champaign, IL: Human Kinetics.

Maslow, A. (2010). *Towards a psychology of being*. Eastford, CT: Martino.

Maw, H, & Maw, E. (1970). Self-concepts of high- and low-curiosity boys. *Child Development, 41*(1), 123–129.

McKenzie, M., & Blenkinsop, S. (2006). An ethic of care and education practice. *Journal of Adventure Education & Outdoor Learning, 6*(2), 91–106.

McKeown, R. (2002). *Education for sustainable development toolkit*. Retrieved from http://www.esdtoolkit.org/

Melaville, A., Berg, A.C., & Blank, M.J. (2006). *Community-based learning: Engaging students for success and citizenship*. Washington, DC: Coalition for Community Schools.

Muñoz, S.A. (2009). *Children in the outdoors: A literature review*. Forres, UK: Sustainable Development Research Centre.

Naess, A. (1989) *Ecology, community and lifestyle*. Cambridge: Cambridge University Press.

National Curriculum. (n.d.). *Physical education key stage 2*. Retrieved from http://curriculum.qcda.gov.uk/key-stages-1-and-2/subjects/physical-education/keystage2/index.aspx

New Zealand Ministry of Education. (2007). *New Zealand curriculum for English-medium teaching and learning in years 1–13*. Wellington: Ministry of Education.

New Zealand Ministry of Education. (2008). *Education outside the classroom guidelines*. Retrieved from http://eotc.tki.org.nz/EOTC-home/EOTC-Guidelines

Nicol, R. (2001). *Outdoor education for sustainable living? An investigation into the potential of Scottish local authority residential outdoor education centres to deliver programmes relating to sustainable living*. PhD Thesis: University of Edinburgh.

Nicol, R., & Higgins, P. (1998). A sense of place: A context for environmental outdoor education. In P. Higgins, & B. Humberstone (Eds), *Celebrating diversity: Learning by sharing cultural differences* (pp. 50–55). Marburg: European Institute for Outdoor Adventure and Experiential Learning.

Nicolazzo, P. (2007). *Effective outdoor program design and management*. Winthrop, WA: Wilderness Medicine Training Centre.

Orr, D. (1992). *Ecological literacy: Education and the transition to a postmodern world*. Albany, NY: State University of New York Press.

Orr, D.W. (2004). *Earth in mind: On education, environment, and the human prospect*. Washington, DC: Island Press.

Outdoor Education Australia. (2010). *The Freemantle Declaration*. Retrieved from http://www.outdooreducationaustralia.org.au/index.htm

Palmer, J., & Suggate, J. (1996). Influences and experiences affecting the pro-environmental behaviour of educators. *Environmental Education* Research, 2(1), 109–121.

Percy-Smith, B., & Malone, K. (2001). Making children's participation in neighbourhood settings relevant to the everyday lives of young people. *PLA Notes, 42*(Oct), 18–22.

Piaget, J. (1977). *The moral judgement of the child*. Middlesex: Penguin.

Piaget, J. (2002). *The language and thought of the child*. London: Routledge.

Priest, S., & Gass, M. (1997). *Effective leadership in adventure programming*. Champaign, IL: Human Kinetics.

Putnam, R. (2000). *Bowling alone: The collapse and revival of American community.* London: Simon & Schuster.

Rickinson, M., Dillon, J., Teamey, K., Morris, M., Choi, M. Y., Sanders, D., & Benefield, P. (2004). *A review of research on outdoor learning.* Shrewsbury: National Foundation for Educational Research and King's College London.

Rogers, C. (1961). *A therapist's view of psychotherapy? On becoming a person.* London: Constable.

Rogers, C. (1983). *Freedom to learn: For the 80s.* London: Merrill.

Ross, H., Higgins, P., & Nicol, R. (2007). Outdoor study of nature: Teachers' motivations and contexts. *Scottish Educational Review, 39*(2), 160-172.

Rovegno, I. (2006). Situated perspectives on learning. In D. Kirk, D. Macdonald, & M. O'Sullivan (Eds), *The handbook of physical education* (262–274). London: Sage.

Rovegno, I., & Dolly, J. (2006) Constructivist perspectives on learning. In D. Kirk, D. Macdonald, & M. O'Sullivan (Eds), *The handbook of physical education* (pp. 242–261). London: Sage.

Rubens, D. (1997). *Outdoor education, adventure and learning: A fusion.* MSc Thesis: University of Edinburgh.

Rubens, D. (1999). Effort or performance: Keys to motivated learners in the outdoors. *Horizons, 4,* 26–28.

Schaffer, H. (2004). *Introducing child psychology.* Oxford: Blackwell.

Scharle, Á., and Szabó A. (2000). *Learner autonomy: A guide to developing learner responsibility.* Cambridge: Cambridge University Press.

Scottish Executive. (2004). *Health and safety on educational excursions: A good practice guide.* Edinburgh: Scottish Executive.

Scottish Government. (n.d.). *Health and safety on educational excursions: A good practice guide.* Retrieved from http://www.scotland.gov.uk/Publications/2004/12/20444/48944

Scottish Government. (2004). *A curriculum for excellence.* Edinburgh: Scottish Government. Retrieved from http://www.scotland.gov.uk/Publications/2004/11/20178/45862

Sharan, Y. (2010). Cooperative learning for academic and social gains: Valued pedagogy, problematic practice. *European Journal of Education, 45*(2), 300–313.

Smith, G. (2002). Learning to be where we are. *Phi Delta Kappan, 83*(8), 584–594.

Smith, G., & Sobel, D. (2010). *Place-and community-based education in schools.* London: Routledge.

Smith, M. (2000). *Curriculum theory and practice: The encyclopaedia of informal education.* Retrieved from http://www.infed.org/biblio/b-curric.htm

Smith, P., Cowie, H., & Blades, M. (1998). *Understanding children's development* (3rd ed). Oxford: Blackwell.

Smyth, J. (1999). Is there a future for education consistent with Agenda 21? *Canadian Journal of Environmental Education, 4,* 69–82.

Sobel, D. (2008). *Childhood and nature: Design principles for educators.* Portland: Stenhouse.

Sparkes, A. (2002). *Telling tales in sport and physical activity: A qualitative journey.* Leeds: Human Kinetics.

Sterling, S. (2001). *Sustainable education: Re-visioning learning and change.* Schumacher Briefings. Bristol: Schumacher UK.

Stetson, C. (n.d). *An essay on Kurt Hahn – founder of Outward Bound.* Unpublished manuscript. Retrieved from http://www.kurthahn.org/writings/stet.pdf

Stewart, A. (2004). Decolonising encounters with the Murray River: Building place responsive outdoor education. *Australian Journal of Outdoor Education, 8*(2), 46–55.

Suzuki, D. (1997). *The sacred balance: Rediscovering our place in nature.* NSW, Australia: Allen and Unwin.

Tierney, W. (1993). The cedar closet. *International Journal of Qualitative Studies in Education, 6*(4), 303–314.

Tilbury, D., & Wortman, D. (Eds.) (2004). *Engaging people in sustainability.* Gland, Switzerland: IUCN.

Titman, W. (1994). *Special places; special people.* Godalming, UK: World Wide Fund for Nature.

Tremmel, J. C., Page, E., & Ott, K. (2009). Editorial – special issue on climate change and intergenerational justice. *Intergenerational Justice Review, 9*(3). Retrieved from http://www.intergenerationaljustice.org/images/stories/IGJR/igjr_09.pdf

UNCED (United Nations Conference on Environment and Development). (1992). *Earth Summit 1992.* London: Regency Press.

UNESCO (United Nations Educational, Scientific and Cultural Organization). (2010). *The UN Decade of Education for Sustainable Development 2005–2014.* Retrieved from http://www.unesco.org/en/esd/

Victorian Curriculum and Assessment Authority. (2005). *Outdoor and environmental studies.* Retrieved from http://www.vcaa.vic.edu.au/vce/studies/outdoor/outdoorenvirostd.pdf

Vygotsky, L. (1978). *Mind in society: The development of higher psychological processes.* Cambridge, MA: Harvard University Press.

Wilber, K. (2000). *Integral psychology.* London: Shambhala.

Willison, J., & O'Regan, K. (2007). Commonly known, commonly not known, totally unknown: A framework for students becoming researchers. *Higher Education Research & Development, 26*(4), 393–409.

Wood, D. (1998). *How children think and learn* (2nd ed). Oxford: Blackwell.

World Commission on Environment and Development. (1987). *Our common future.* Oxford: Oxford University Press.

World Health Organization. (2009). *WHO guidelines on hand hygiene in health care.* http://whqlibdoc.who.int/publications/2009/9789241597906_eng.pdf

Index